T0095163

If Not For The Horses

Horses

Joe Klemm

Order this book online at www.trafford.com
or email orders@trafford.com

Most Trafford titles are also available at major online book retailers.

© Copyright 2011 Joe Klemm.
All rights reserved. No part of this publication may be reproduced, stored in a retrieval
system, or transmitted, in any form or by any means, electronic, mechanical, photocopying,
recording, or otherwise, without the written prior permission of the author.

Printed in the United States of America.

ISBN: 978-1-4269-5854-0 (sc)
ISBN: 978-1-4269-5853-3 (e)

Trafford rev. 02/24/2011

 www.trafford.com

North America & international
toll-free: 1 888 232 4444 (USA & Canada)
phone: 250 383 6864 ♦ fax: 812 355 4082

DEDICATION

My heartfelt thanks to Neil and Renate Harrelson, who patiently translated my scribble (or chicken scratch) and put it on the computer. To my children, who helped proofread and gave me the encouragement and support to see this through - Chris Klemm, Monica Bourdlaies and Debbie Beardslee; and special thanks to Dr. Ingert Kuzych for all the time and effort he took to proofread, while in the midst of his own crisis.

Introduction

As we approached Oldenstadt in north Germany, I began reflecting on how it had all begun and how we had managed to get this far west. Mainly, however, I missed my home in Lithuania, my dad, and my 16-year-old brother, Johann.

It had been so pleasant living in our log farmhouse, sleeping in my own bed, with mom making breakfast. But by now I had had enough of loudmouth SS men, enough of uniforms, of explosives, dirt, gravel, shrapnel, and the smell of gunpowder. I dreamt once more of our lilac hedge and jasmine bushes along the fence in mom's garden and of her fresh baked bread.

We had been forced to leave it all behind. Dictator Stalin of Russia and dictator Hitler of Germany arranged a Non-Aggression Pact between the Soviet Union and Germany in 1939 that included a secret protocol dividing Eastern Europe between them. Stalin said he'd take the countries from Finland on the Baltic in the north to Romania by the Black Sea in the south. Hitler agreed, but with the stipulation that the German people, descendants of the folks Queen Catherine had settled in these countries in the 18th century to modernize them, would be returned to Germany. (Additionally, Hitler also claimed about two-thirds of Poland for an expanded Germany.) So that was how our lives were changed forever. Surviving between two brutal dictators was, to say the least, very frightening. It is unpleasant to relive the next six tumultuous years; yet I would like to tell my story of survival which, at times, I found exciting, frightening, and – believe it or not—occasionally fun.

CHAPTER 1

One day in 1939, Mrs. Bubniene, our neighbor, came to us all excited. She had the only radio in the region, and had heard that the Russians were coming. "They will take over Lithuania and we won't be a free county anymore," she lamented. The next day, Stankewitsius, another neighbor, told us that the Russians were already moving on Marijampole.

First the Russian soldiers came, then their wives and children on little horse-drawn wagons. No more Lithuanian newspapers, no more Lithuanian radio. Slowly, the Russians tightened their grip on us all. Lithuanian President, Smetona, fled to Germany and from there to the United States; it was in Cleveland that someone burned him to death in his son's apartment. Some professors disappeared; the Russians would come at night and load up the trucks with political dissidents, with wealthier or influential people, or with folks of German descent and haul them off to Russia or Siberia.

Things got worse. We all lived in fear that we might be next but, fortunately, we were just little dogs on our little farm so we got to stay for a while. Soon a red-haired, loud-mouthed farmhand, Rudis (meaning "red"), who never owned anything before the Russians arrived, now came to strut about with a hammer and sickle medallion on his lapel. This emblem allowed him to tell dad and other farmers when to work and when not to work—such as on a Russian holiday. He had the authority to report us and have us hauled away. We complied with all the rules and stayed on the farm in fear.

One nice, sunny June day mom was fishing in our pond. Mom had the newest style swimsuit on, one-piece, with thighs exposed. (Mom was a modern woman, the other farm wives would cover the thighs to the knees and even the arms to the elbows.) I was sitting next to the pail and playing with the fish she had caught. She took a large potato basket, held it in one hand and paddled with the other hand and feet across the pond. Each time she caught a few. That's when a well-dressed gentleman came to see us. He said he was sent by the German Government to register us so we could go to Germany if we wanted. There was an agreement with the Russians that we would not get shot or hauled off to Siberia for that. We could go when the Germans got the train into Vilkowiskai. We could even pack suitcases. They would not be confiscated. But we would have to leave the farm and everything in it, and we could not sell anything before leaving. Those were the rules.

When dad arrived home from the neighbor's farm, mom told him the rules. They cried and then laughed cynically; the two dictators had hundreds of thousands of us little dogs in their palms. All our parents' life savings and grandpa's also were wrapped up in the farm, but mom and dad decided to leave as they were of German descent and the family would have a better chance at freedom in Germany. The Russians would have found a reason to confiscate our land and transport us to Siberia and we knew what agonies some suffered in that process. Mother's sister-in-law died in Russia after WWI and her husband escaped from Siberia. He was one of thousands of people from Lithuania who had been deported to Siberia during WWI.

So early one morning in the spring of 1940 we drove off with our horse and buggy to the train station in Vilkowiskai, 18 km

(11 mi) away. We left the livestock and warm house. Mom was crying and the yard dog, left on a chain, was also crying. Dad just looked straight ahead. I could not tell if he was crying; I had never seen him cry. As for me, I was already thinking of the train ride and of going to another country. I had heard of Germany and its beautiful castles and 1,200-year old cities. It was sad to leave all my peers and my home, but anxious to "go and see what's ahead."

Papers were checked and we boarded the train. In a few hours we were across the German border. There was a brass band from the Lithuanian city of Kaunas playing happy tunes. We could debark from the train to get coffee and cake and then get back on. We rode all day across East Prussia to West Prussia, an area that had been disputed by the Germans and Poles over the last 800 to 900 years. We arrived in Preusse Stargard and stayed in a former "insane asylum" for about three months. It was a very clean place and resembled a park-like college campus. There was a big mess hall and no one went hungry. I kept wondering, however, why the Germans were putting us up like this.

Dad and all the other able-bodied men left us for another place in East Prussia called Neidenburg. There they assisted in assembling the pre-fabricated barracks for displaced people from Lithuania.

Several days prior, we were informed that the 20th of April was Hitler's birthday. Everyone was expected to participate in the festivities. What a disappointing party that turned out to be!

At 10 a.m. on the big day we were grouped by age. The "Frauenschaft," (the mothers), the girls, the old men, and then groups of boys from 17 to 7 years were each assembled. We marched for an hour in Preusse Stargard city. Then Hitler started barking for 1½ to 2 hours over very loud speakers hooked up all over Germany. We had been told before leaving to go to the bathroom; there would not be another chance for us until we returned in the afternoon. Everyone had to march, there had to be a big showing. The streets were lined with red swastika flags and no traffic was allowed. We marched about twenty boys abreast across the whole street. The city square was filled with the SA, the brownshirts. The "Gauleiter," a Nazi big-shot, saluted the units as they marched by. We boys then listened and waited on the side streets. I heard (rather than saw) large units doing the goosestep and brass bands playing marching music. Groups bellowed "Sieg Heil" three times and finally the party was over. We then marched back for another hour. What a crappy party. We had marched and stood, got nothing to drink, were dry mouthed and tired. I hoped never again to attend another event like it.

One day we were loaded on a train and taken to the city of Neidenburg in East Prussia (which borders Lithuania). The barracks had been completed. They smelled awful, of tar – carboleneum – and had a lot of itchy glass wool or fiberglass insulation that escaped through the wood cracks. Our barracks were just two miles from the center of Neidenburg, an old German city overlooked by an ancient castle on top of a hill. The barracks were enclosed by a high wire fence, topped off with four rows of barbed wire. The front gate was overseen by an Army or SS guy who sat and watched the comings and goings. We were free to go anywhere without asking.

Each family was assigned one room. Our room had two double bunk beds and one single bed, one crude table, two stools, and one bench. There was one coal heater the size of a five gallon bucket which kept the room warm in the winter. The hall or walkway was in the center of the barracks with a door at each end. There was also one large room with toilets and a laundry room at one end. However, there were no showers, no tubs, and no hot water. Instead there was a round, fountain-like tub with a foot pedal that squirted water from its fountain. One could choose to take a sponge bath or smell "au naturel."

The barrack number would be announced over the loudspeaker for its turn to eat in the mess hall. They had large kettles for the soup, which was served with a slice of dark rye bread. We sure hated that food but that's all we got. In the morning we could pick up chicory coffee and hard rolls from the mess hall. The hard rolls were my favorite. We could not cook in our rooms.

Another odd thing was the lack of young men. They were being trained for the army. Since my dad was 45 years old, he could stay with us. He sometimes pondered aloud and discussed with our Lithuanian neighbors, What would Hitler want next? He had already taken Poland and most of France, occupied some other small countries like Holland and Belgium, and had annexed Austria, parading in after his Army in his convertible. What more did he want? I wondered if Hitler's nasty Gestapo guys had arranged the welcome by the thousands of Austrians waving the swastika flags along the route—with everyone screaming "Sieg Heil"—the same way we were forced to go to his birthday parade in Preusse Stargard?

My dad was assigned the job of keeping the Red Cross barrack heated. It was run by the Army. A nun was in charge of the nursery there and a doctor would sometimes attend. The barrack had three boilers and dad would shovel the coke and watch the gauges. These were the duties he was expected to perform—without pay, of course. Everything now belonged to the Reich.

Nonetheless, no one wanted to return to Lithuania because the Russians were deporting the farmers to Siberia. Since they had been landowners, they were deemed unreliable and had to work in the mines for eight to ten years. A very high percentage of these honest farmers never returned. My cousin Theo was able to get away. He was Aunt Minna's son, had a college degree, and was gifted in languages, knowing English, Russian, French, German, and Lithuanian. He did a lot of writing for the Russian occupation forces of Lithuania. They could not do everything with their machine guns. He wrote proclamations and new laws for the Russians who were now occupying the former free countries. At night they would lock him and his friends in jail, but during the day he worked in their offices.

Germany had not had a free press for a long time and now it was also true in Lithuania. I don't know how Theo escaped but he made it to the barracks and there explained to dad how Hitler had taken over Germany by force. The farmers did not have access to newspapers and would get the news from hearsay in Lithuania.

So we learned from Theo that when President Hindenburg died, the German people wanted to vote for a new chancellor and president. Hitler, who was then the chancellor, did not want a vote. That upset the intelligencia of Munich. The good Bavarians quickly organized a large demonstration, clamoring for voting rights and marching by the thousands to the steps of the Feldherrenhalle—the seat of the Bavarian Government. Hitler's brownshirts appeared on the high steps of that building, overlooking the Square. They set up heavy machine guns and cut down many of the demonstrators. Some citizens fled to the side streets, but were picked up by the truckloads and taken to concentration camps. Hitler went on the radio and proclaimed himself leader (Fuehrer). As a side note, he mentioned that the traitors and saboteurs in Munich had been caught and killed.

Uncle Theo told my father, "If you want to live you have to shut up, otherwise you might end up like the good Bavarians." Dad became serious and quit laughing and joking about the paperhanger (Hitler). There could have been Gestapo informers among us in the camp.

So much for Neidenburg. I actually was able to attend the school there now that I was eight years old. I had previously attended only six to seven weeks of school in Lithuania before we left. I could read stories and write with my brothers when they did homework. Mom said my reading and writing was nice, but she made no big deal about it. In Neidenburg the teacher took me aside and drew a funny looking letter. It looked Chinese to me but it was in Gothic script, which I had not seen before. I was glad no one could laugh at me. He asked how I wrote the letters, and after I showed him, he said that my letters were the Latin script. I got used to the "new" alphabet quickly and also soon adapted to the high-German speech. I did not want the people to think me a "foreigner."

Chapter 2

Unexpectedly, in the late spring or early summer of 1941, thousands of soldiers marched past our barracks day and night. They marched up to the Lithuanian border where the Russians were. Then bang, one morning, the Blitzkrieg was on. In just a few days, the Russians were removed from Lithuania. The tanks, cannons, and troops just kept moving east. There seemed to be no end. The large loudspeakers all over the compound never quit blasting the news of the victories in the east, and the tonnage sunk in the oceans by the U-Boats.

On the other hand, all I could think about was scraping out the marmalade buckets that were thrown out of the mess hall. I loved marmalade. I would sing "Marmeladeneimer" (marmalade bucket).

Next, we were shipped out quite suddenly to the Polish city of Ilowa. The Reich needed our barracks for thousands of French war prisoners. They worked in the town wherever needed, but at night had to return to the camp. I was glad to leave the camp, but in Poland I had no toys or no wheels of any kind. I was in a new school, an old three story building, and felt very unwanted.

The hate was great here between the Germans and the Poles. They had had wars with one another for hundreds of years. They looked at me as if they wanted to kill me. I was a foreigner here again. In our mess hall in the middle of the town hung the swastika flag, which showed everyone who was in charge here.

Now dad worked on a furniture truck, helping to deliver furniture to the Germans all over Poland that Hitler had planted there so that it would become a German region quickly. Sure enough, many Polish families took on German citizenship.

My Aunt Wanda, who was not so young anymore, had a baby boy in Neidenburg. She named him Gerhard. He was a cute baby with red hair. His brother Ewald was 17 at the time and could soon be drafted into the army.

The summer of 1942 came. We were still in Ilowa and occasionally I was allowed to accompany dad and the driver to different locales in Poland and West Prussia. I stood in the back of the truck seeing new cities and villages and wishing the drive would last all day, the trips were always over too soon.

Then the big news came: We were going back to Lithuania! Man, was I happy! I recited the names of all our neighbors in Shirwiedai within one mile or less: Bindokas, Stankiewicius, Lepshies, General Valowich, Adele Bubnicue, Zdanies, and Kurevicius. I could not wait to see them all and tell them of all the places I had been. So, one morning, they loaded all of us on a freight train and back we went to Lithuania. We were all filled with anxiety. How would our farm look? What about the buildings? What animals were left? By night we arrived in Kaunas, the second largest city, only 45 minutes from our home.

We soon found out, however, that we would not be going back to our own farm. Instead, the Reich needed German people in the Polish section of Lithuania. After sitting around for weeks in Kaunas in a forcefully vacated convent, in a big hall with lots of bunks, a Lithuanian farmer came with a field wagon and horses and drove us in the opposite direction of our home. We ended up going to Vandzogala – I hated that name – and a three-farm village called Bonishkai. The farm they assigned us was situated in the lowlands. The roads were muddy and the farm was muddy. The straw roofs of the house and the barn had holes in them.

In the house sat a fat Russian soldier, a prisoner of war, assigned to work on what was now "our farm." The original owner had been removed just because he was of Polish descent; that's how it is when you live under a dictatorship. There had been plenty of Germans living in the region of our original farm, but there were not enough Germans living here in this new locale, so that's why we were transplanted.

Everything was always arranged for us, we had no say in the matter. Never were we asked, "How would you like that?" We were a sad family sitting in this dark, bare house. We had little in our suitcases. We needed a whole kitchen. We had no food.

Mom and I went to the closest new neighbor, a very large landowner—actually three brothers with their families. I could count approximately fifty horses, some used for plowing. Some were real beauties, tall and sleek, long—necked Hannoveraners. A few were of the British variety. The brothers did not hitch those to a fancy buggy or a landau. If the Germans had them they would have proudly displayed them – riding in uniform in a parade. The brothers kept them for use on the farm.

Well, the nice neighbors fixed us up with home-baked bread, bacon, and eggs, which tied us over till we were able to get back to Kaunas with our horse team for some shopping. You could not buy what you wanted; instead, you bought what was available. We did get flour at the German PX or commissary.

Once in a while a party man in his SA brown uniform would come to the farm; his name was Herr Apfel (Mr. Apple). He would bring a cow or a horse to the farm to make it more productive. He was in charge of all the German farms in the area. In a short time we had planted potatoes, wheat, and rye.

In the meantime, we got another German neighbor, Herr Kalpin. He was very heavy, had a big mouth, and always walked with a rifle in his hand. He was a "Stutzpunkleiter," more like a messenger for the Nazi regime. He thought he was *the* big shot in the area because of his position within the regime. I always felt sorry for his nice, quiet wife. They seemed such a mismatch. They had a real bratty son my age too.

Pretty soon Kalpin came around with a brown uniform and a shotgun for my father. Dad laughed at him and said he would not wear it. Well, he told dad to have it on for Sunday morning at Berger's farm in Vandzogala. Some big shots from the Reich would be there and whoever did not follow the rules:

"Well, you know, Gustav, when the Gestapo comes you know where you'll be going." So dad put it on Sunday morning. He looked so stupid in that brown uniform, but I bit my tongue and said nothing. He wore a trench coat over it and got on the wagon. I hopped on also, wanting to see the old farmers in their uniforms.

We arrived before 10 a.m. The big shot in charge took down names and compared these with his list. Some farmers came late at 10:30 a.m., just like to an old town meeting. The big shot lined them up and had them run up and down on the farmyard. He stood there in his green SS uniform, with a pistol in a holster, shiny boots, and mouth wide open blaring orders. The farmers were slowly getting tired and quietly cussing. All were over 45, since the young had already all been drafted. He told them that they now belonged to the Reich and that it would not be long and they would all be wearing the uniform, fighting for the Fatherland. The farmers were not happy, but they had no choice. So it was set, every 14 days they had to be there for a "meeting."

Back on the farm, life got a bit better. Pauras, one of the brothers on the neighboring farm, had two sons, Jonas and Juosas. (My name was also Juosas in Lithuanian. In Poland, it was Juzu, and in our house it was Josef.) We boys got along fine.

We would ride their horses home in the evening after a long day's work—it always turned out to be a race for a mile or two. We ran up to the sleek horses and swung ourselves on their backs. No reins, no saddles, we most often rode bareback. We had them gallop quickly since a fast trot would shake us up and hurt the hinder – especially when they did the long high jumps over the ditches. Some would slow up just before they'd jump and we would come down on the hump by their necks and that would hurt. The horses always knew the direction to the trough filled with cold well water. Old man Paurus would come out and give us the devil for getting the horses too hot and not giving them enough time to cool down before putting them away, but by the next evening his words would be forgotten and we would race again, all the way to the watering trough.

Our Russian farm helper, Mikalai Ossipov, also became my friend. He taught me a lot of Russian and was good in handwriting. He was, however, slow on the farm. When he was plowing with a double-bottom plough – three horses – I would go out to the fields and walk behind him. After a while he would hit the grass and snooze; walking on the soft earth made the heavy man very tired. He told me he had been a train station director in Moscow. He also said that when the Germans finally lost the war, I should come to Moscow and he would take good care of me. But I was dreaming of the West where dad was when he was young, of the Rhine, the pretty castles, and the old towns. Dad said there were no muddy roads there. I hated mud. On this farm we had too much of it.

Herr Apfel sent a team of workers who put up a new shingle roof on our house, plastered the inside, and painted it. By now the farm was running pretty well. We had sheep, cows, turkeys, chickens, and ducks. Dad worked and cooperated with the Lithuanian neighbors. When winter came, I would get up at 6 a.m. and ride our team of horses to the neighbor's and hitch them to the circular machine with four crossbeams—each for two horses to pull. I would stand on the platform in the center of this six-foot diameter wood-covered gear, and keep a constant speed with the eight horses. In the barn, the turning thrashing machine drum would howl like a siren. I loved speed.

I was now ten or eleven years old and had control of eight horses! It was just too bad they had to walk in a circle. I never got anywhere but at night I got to ride home in the dark with my two

11

fairly closely matched horses. I also had a young dog who was half-German shepherd. He looked just like a shepherd but was smaller and happier than big shepherds that always look so serious. My little dog ran next to the horses and never barked. Sometimes the moon shone on the snowfields and I could see for one or two miles. But other times, when it was cloudy or foggy, I would rely on my dog and my horses to get me home safely.

One night, only three miles from home, as I approached a cluster of trees, my shepherd started to growl and ran faster—so did I with my horses. I knew that there were thousands of partisans in the Lithuanian woods. Some were Communists, some patriots, and some were escaped Russian war prisoners who had just walked off the farms. The others were Russian Army deserters. They all had to eat and would come to the farms, mostly the German ones, kill and cut up a cow, load it on their horses, and take whatever else was available, all in the name of survival. They would come into the farmer's homes and keep the entire family and farm helpers facing the wall as the others in the group would round up what was needed. By the next morning they would be far away. The nearest police post was in Kaunas, 30 miles away. You could hitch the wagon and ride there to tell the authorities – they'd listen and write down your complaint, but had no men to go after them.

All the German men were scattered throughout Western Europe, France, North Africa, Egypt, Greece, Ukraine, and – the greatest number – in Russia. About one-third were already dead, missing, or locked away as prisoners in Siberian mines. Now I know why the German Government issued rifles and shotguns to the farmers. Dad, however, never once used his. He just remained on good terms with all his neighbors and, I think, if the partisans had raided our farm, he would have helped them pack the stuff they wanted.

CHAPTER 3

One night my parents were invited to a farm down the road past Paura's farm to a kind of Thanksgiving party; it was held after all the thrashing and butchering on the farms had been completed for the year. It was a Saturday night get-together for all to attend, helpers and neighbors were all invited. In Lithuanian it is called "Talka." Dad took his happy button accordion and walked there with mom. As they were sitting at the table, the door flew open and Mr. Kalpin stepped in and shot into the ceiling with the gun he was carrying. Dust and plaster fell into the food and drinks on the table. Everyone was shocked. Mr. Kalpin announced the law:

"No parties with foreigners." That meant my dad should not associate socially with the Lithuanian neighbors. Mother said she had never seen dad killing-mad in all her life. Dad ran Kalpin out of the kitchen and down the road. When he came close, Kalpin held dad off by pointing his gun at him, saying he was only doing his duty and that dad should not be mad at him. Kalpin kept talking like that as he was chased all the way to our farm. Then dad quickly dove into our house and came out with *his* shotgun. You should have seen that barrel-with-legs run home!

Kalpin was very jealous of us, we had made so many friends and he and his gun not a single one. About a week later, dad had to report to Gestapo headquarters in Kaunas regarding this incident. Kalpin, the accuser, told his story first. Dad, still mad, told the Gestapo that he delivered grain. All our neighbors delivered what the government required and none of our barns were being burned down by the partisans. We were doing the best we could to survive among the partisans and extend a friendly, helping hand to our Lithuanian neighbors and Kalpin was not helping with his threats. Dad continued, "I have nephews fighting in the Kaukasus' frozen tundra and some have already died, some froze to death like my brother-in-law, Rudolf Wainowski, because they did not get winter clothing."

The Gestapo man did not like the last remark but he said, "Mr. Klemm, calm down, this kind of talk could get you a train ride into the Reich." Turning to Kalpin he said, "Herr Kalpin, you are a Schweinhund, going into a neighbor's house and shooting into the ceiling." He continued, "I want you two to make up right now and I want to see you run good farms and not have Mr. Klemm sent to a concentration camp, we need him here."

When dad got home we all laughed for joy because we were so relieved to have him back with us.

We asked, "What did the Gestapo say?" "Kalpin, du bist ein Schweinhund," he told us. That was as bad as the worst insult.

Uncle Albert Klemm's farm was about 6 miles away from ours. One day mom baked cookies for her younger brother Rudolf Wainowski. He was on the front lines in Russia. Uncle Albert and Aunt Wanda would be going to the post office in Kaunas the following day. I was to take the package to Aunt Wanda by 5 a.m. before they left for town. I could hardly wait to get on my favorite fast Palomino look-alike horse. I was trotting along nicely and carefully so as not to get into a ditch when I saw someone smoking up ahead. Whoever it was, however, heard me. When I came up to where they'd been, the cigarettes and people were only shadows. I cut loose with my horse into a real wild gallop all the way to Aunt Wanda's farm. On the way, about two miles from my destination, I passed a burning barn. No people were around since no one would ever come out of the house to put out the fire. One could get killed that way. The partisans burned the barns for revenge. I waited for daylight to ride back, still a bit scared. Aunt Wanda was angry with my father and me for letting me ride at night, but I was the one who'd wanted to. My brother, Al, was not quite as adventurous. Brother Johann (John) was always in Kaunas at high school.

Uncle Rudolf, mother's youngest brother, never received the cookies. He died at the front lines a month before Christmas. I will always miss him. When he visited us on furlough he would speak Russian with me. I was happy that he could understand me with what I learned from our Mikalai. Uncle Rudolf told me never to forget any of the languages I'd learned (German, Lithuanian, or Russian). He would tell me that I would get along much better in this world if I held onto them. Later, in Germany, I strove to sound just as the natives because there, the minute they detected a foreign accent, you became a second-class person.

My parents finally went to visit our former home area. Uncle Herman Klemm, dad's youngest brother, lived on the Josef Klemm farm, that of my deceased grandfather. Uncle Herman had married a Lithuanian girl, and that was who my parents stayed with. Uncle Herman and his wife had stayed behind when the Russians came, because she did not want to go to Germany. Al and I could not accompany our parents so we stayed home with a maid, Stevka, a farmhand, Petras, and Mikalai Ossipov, the Russian. My parents had to get a travel permit, a "Passagierschein," from Kaunas. All the information needed was on it; who, what, when, where, why, and how. You could not deviate from that. Everything was tightly controlled by the Wehrmacht. When they arrived at the farm, the buildings were gone. Hitler had taken several mid-sized farms and assigned one Lithuanian-born German to administer them. It was much more productive that way.

For three months that summer, I even attended school. We did not have a regular teacher but instead two workforce girls,

"Arbeitsmaid," in uniforms from Germany. They might have graduated from high school. We had no textbooks. They brought with them a box full of Grimm's fairytales that we used for reading. All the children there had been born in Lithuania and spoke German. It was fun being with them and listening to their Prussian dialect, but my time with them only lasted for a few months.

Chapter 4

One day in early June of 1944, Kalpin came to our farm on official business, but this time without his gun. He said we should consider gathering our belongings and be prepared to leave at a moments notice. By this time the German war effort in Russia was failing and if the Army could not turn back the advancing Russians, we would be overrun and trapped under Russian control.

He then had a big favor to ask of dad, could Johann ride to warn all of the German farmers in Kalpin's region? He was actually begging. We all knew that we could not just get up and leave under this strict dictatorship, so it made sense to try and be accommodating.

My ears perked up. I asked if I could go instead of my brother and would I be able to use that nice mare of Kalpin's for the ride? He said I could take any of his horses to deliver the message. He himself could not go. We all knew he would be killed by any of the partisans or the good Lithuanians that he had abused. Now would be their chance to get even.

Well, dad knew of many good farmers who needed to be notified, so he gave in and let me ride the region since I had the best chance. None of the partisans or Lithuanians had killed children – at least not that we knew of. Mikalai had told dad that his Russian comrades would return to reclaim this area sooner or later, but my father dismissed this as a boast.

I was really feeling good. I could ride and ride, day after day. I knew the dikes I had to cross by Jonava, thirty km away along the river. One day I was just an hour's ride from home when a young Lithuanian stepped out of the woods into my path. He was at least 17 and I was only 11½ years old, so he looked grown up to me. I did not take off. He looked friendly and abased, looking down and kicking gravel with his shoe as he greeted me.

He said, "You're Juosas."

I said, "Yes."

He continued, "I've been sent to ask you about the orders you are carrying to all the farmers. Is it true that when you all leave you will be burning all the farms and fields?"

I responded, "That's not true. We are supposed to tie two of our biggest Holstein cows behind the horse wagon and go west to Wilkija by the Memel River. There we are to gather on the meadows about two km before the church on the river banks. The army engineers will build a floating bridge there. That's all."

He thanked me and told me that he had heard about me. I certainly did not know him, but he was such a pleasant fellow— one who could have been a friend instantly. He might have been with the underground and working by day somewhere. He wanted to shake my hand, so I did, and he wished me well. He also said that both of us should expect the war to arrive, and who knew what would happen then. I bade him well and told him that we would leave before the Russians came.

He said, "This is my home and if I were to go to Russia or Germany I would be a stranger." We parted. I rode home slowly, deep in thought. It was a sad situation.

CHAPTER 5

As it happened, the German Army kept the Russians out of Lithuania. April and May went by and we were busy planting and sowing. Then came June and we harvested the first cut of hay from the meadows.

My brother Johann came home from Kaunas. He said that the people from there were leaving for the West because the Russians had broken through. Dad did not want to leave now. He was sitting high on a hay wagon; a bee had stung him on his eyebrow just a few minutes before, and he could hardly see with the swollen eye. He was moaning loudly.

"Now that I've worked again for over two years, day and night, have animals, planted the fields, and gotten the house in shape, now I have to leave." He was almost crying.

Then Mikalai, the Russian, came out of the house in his Russian uniform. He said to me, "Sluhai, Jusu, (Listen, Joe), I have to go now, back to the prison camp. Don't forget what I told you about Moscow. At any railroad station there, I'll pick you up." With a tear in his eye, we parted. Dad did not see Mikalai off; he didn't want to hear him say, "I told you so."

We unloaded the hay wagon but kept some for the two cows and the horses that we would be taking with us. The bulk, though, was set aside. In the house, mom unfolded a tablecloth and piled underwear and linens on it. Then, tying it into a bundle, she threw it on the wagon. We did the same with our shoes and the few clothes we had. Dad took his shotgun but left his hated brown uniform.

He said, "What more can they do to me?"

Chapter 6

It was mid-afternoon on a warm June day in 1944, and the sun was shining brightly. The farm was alive again with an abundance of livestock and all the hard work that had gone into making this a prosperous farm. Now, again, we were leaving it all behind. Juosas and Jonas Pauras waved good-bye to us from afar. It was not good for them to be seen talking with us at this time. Collaborating with "The Enemy" would get you sent to the salt mines in Siberia. The Communist civilians might have been watching already, and they would surely report such activity. The Russians were close and would be there soon.

With every mile we rode, I started feeling better. I was dreaming of some nice places and new horizons, but it was still sad to leave my friends, the animals, and especially my dog.

On the third day, we arrived just below Wikije on the east bank of the Memel River, just as we'd been instructed. On the highest hill above the riverbank stood a beautiful church, which we'd already spotted from a great distance away. We all stayed in the lower part of the city on a large, flat meadow next to the river. Here we found Aunt Wanda Klemm with her family, as well as hundreds of other wagons. The atmosphere was that of a country market. There were rows and rows of wagons with unhitched horses and cows chewing hay. People stood in clusters and discussed what they had been up to over the past two years. We had not seen some of these folks since the barracks of Neidenburg and Prussia.

"See, Juosi, we are Fluechtlinge (refugees, DPs) again," said Aunt Wanda.

We were escaping Communism, but I did not see anybody crying. It was easier to leave the second time. We had to stay at Wikije for three days, since the special work group had to finish the ferry for our crossing. The river water here flowed fast and furiously; it was only 100 km to the Baltic Sea.

CHAPTER 7

My brother Al and I were allowed to ride our two matched mares to the river and give them a bath; it was really fun. We rode bare-back to the fast river. The two mares swam downstream with us and then got out.

Mr. Kalpin watched us and asked me, "Would you take my black stallion for a swim?"

"Of course," I said.

I could hardly wait to get on that black beauty. With hundreds of farmers watching me, I galloped on that steed into the water which, at that spot, was especially deep. I figured that I would swim just like with my mares. But to my astonishment and fright, the stallion's head went under water. I floated next to him and held onto his mane close to his ears and tried to pull the rein and point him to the bank. His hind legs, however, were flailing, so when he caught some ground he shot up like a whale. He coughed, water came out of his nostrils, and his eyes looked white and wild. He made two more underwater hops and finally grabbed some bottom with his front hooves. The minute he leveled off I was on his back. With both my hands now holding on to his thick curly black mane, he started to gallop uncontrollably in water up to his chest. When we got onto solid ground, he sped off like a locomotive, with water squirting from his open mouth. Finally, about a mile downstream, I was able to slow him down and get him back under control. I turned him around and we headed back to camp.

A big crowd had gathered on the bank, anxious about me. Kalpin was furious and started hollering, "If you had drowned my stallion, I would have beaten you to a pulp."

My father came up just then and pulled me off the horse. I think he might have hugged me. As we started to walk away, he turned to Kalpin and, with all the men around, he said, "You are lucky to be alive now. If Jusi and your stupid horse had not come out of the water, you would also be floating downstream with them, dead." Dad did not say anything more as we walked back to our wagon, but I think he was proud of me and the way I handled myself in the wild waters of the Nemunas River.

The next morning, I talked my brother Al into walking with me into city of Wilkije. It was a beautiful June day. We walked around the Catholic Church. It was quiet in the churchyard, which had a clear view up and down the river. The town was small; every street was filled with ladder wagons.

We even found some kids we knew from the three months of school in Vandzogala. We had a lot to talk about and it felt good to hear other people talking to us in the familiar East Prussian dialect. To me this was a great time again. I had no fear, no worry; mom took care of everything and we were once again on the move. This was indeed an exciting time in my life.

By now the ferry was completed and the approaches were built. Al and I watched each farmer handling his team as he drove onto the ferry. My brother Johann was 15 years old now and he was running with the older boys. All the boys 16 and older were gone, pressed into some kind of service. Some of my friends and cousins were already dead at the Russian front. Cousin Ewald Klemm was in the army and still alive, but Aunt Wanda worried about him constantly.

After we crossed the river we had to wait another two days until the rest of the refugees had crossed. We were all instructed to stop at a German border town with a railroad station. When we arrived at our destination, there were a lot of German Army uniforms to be seen. They were not there to greet us; however, they were there to give us some very bad news.

We were informed that dad and his team of horses were now the property of the German Army. There was no arguing. Every man younger than 52 years was in.

"Well, Jousi," he said to me, "Take care of yourself, Al, Johann, and mom. I'll see you when they let me go."

The cows were also taken away and we were loaded onto a freight train. Everything went by in a blur. Dad was gone and the train was moving before mom could even dry her tears. Uncle Albert accompanied us on the train; he was too old for the service. After a long, slow train ride across East Prussia, we ended up in Kulm, by the Weichsel (Wisla) River, in West Prussia.

Here we stayed in barracks that had been constructed in this old city. A few days later, horse wagons appeared by the hundreds to take us to our next destination. We were assigned to Franz Krentz of Duebeln in Kulm County. We threw our belongings on a wagon that was driven by Mr. Plit, a Polish man who had married a German woman. He was the foreman of Krentz's farm. He asked us if we knew anything about farm work and we said that we did. He told us that we had to get to work now. We immediately took a dislike to him. I enjoyed work but I did not like his "you must work" attitude.

Chapter 8

We rode the horse wagon for a day and arrived on the farm late in the afternoon. We saw very clean fields, well-kept orchards, and nice Holstein cows. The Krentz house was made of red brick and so were the barns. All had tiled roofs. We drove through a gate with high, brick posts. The left one bore the warning metal shield reading "Bissige Hunde" (vicious dogs). There was a bright metal shield wrapped around its post. One day I snuck up there and unrolled the shield. Yes sir, just as I thought, "mozney cref," the same meaning, only in Polish. Whichever power ruled at the time, that's whose shield was exposed.

Mr. Krentz was a serious man. He would say hello but never asked how we were, how long we had been traveling, or where is your father? Mrs. Krentz was friendlier. She greeted my mother and told her that she had a three-month old baby daughter. She said she would seek mom's advice, since mom had had three of us. I liked Mrs. Krentz because she would at least smile at us.

Mrs. Krentz was a good cook and also had a Polish girl named Claira to assist her. There was also Frieda who was a friendly, happy, 16-year-old blond German girl from Kulmsee. She had been working at the Krentz's farm for a year, having been placed there by the dictatorship. This was the rule: every girl, after finishing grade school or middle school, had to put in one year of work on a farm or other concern away from home. It was called the "Pflichtjahr" or duty year. The girls learned to cook and do chores and this was done without pay. Everybody worked for the Reich. Everyone was on a list and accounted for. Mr. Plit worked the fields, and Stashy milked the cows. Stashy Orlovski, a former postal employee, had a big family; he was assigned by the dictatorship to work as a farmhand on the Krentz farm. He had a son my age who became my friend. I had to learn Polish fast, for they did not care to learn to speak German.

Life on the farm was pretty boring. We could not touch the horses or anything else. Mr. Plit and Mr. Krentz saw to that. Mr. Krentz was gone a lot at night. The Orlovskis gained my confidence and told me all about Mr. Krentz.

When the Germans attacked Poland, many German civilian men were killed on the Polish side by the Poles. Mr. Krentz's brother was killed in Bromberg by Polish civilians before the Germans took over the city. And so the hate went on.

Mr. Krentz would saddle up his tallest, prettiest horse and throw a black blanket over its back with silver "SS" embroidered on each side. Later, I got a look at his uniform; all black with a high cap and a silver skull on it. Yes, he belonged to the "Waffen SS." These men were hardly ever seen on the front lines but always stayed behind, terrorizing people. We were sure that when he went out at night he was not going out to a party or otherwise socializing.

Al and I decided to go by train to Kulm to visit Aunt Wanda. My cousin Ruth was gone now, working for the Red Cross in Malente, in northern Germany, treating the wounded. In Kulm, we walked every street, which was not very interesting. But the train ride turned out to be very exciting. People from all over were traveling. The countryside we passed was varied and cities and villages flew by. Wow, that really beat sitting on the farm.

By now, my brother Johann had to leave. His high school was situated on the peninsula of Hela in the Baltic Sea in the north of East Prussia. I told him I would accompany him all the way there and then return. It was always OK with mom, she was never afraid for me. We had half a suitcase full of Reichsmark with us. I don't think dad or mom ever counted them. All the stuff on the farm that we sold in Lithuania for the German Reich or Lithuania was paid to us in Marks, but we could not buy anything with them. If I wanted new shoes it was always, "sorry we are all out of them." That was the story with everything but food – for that we had ration cards. So when I traveled, I would order with my ration card and plenty of Marks.

On the way back, I had to go via Graudenz, but the train stopped before the city which was just then being bombed. That was excitement. But a couple hours later, when we slowly glided into the main station, it was quite a sad picture. Another train was all torn up and dead and wounded were being carried out of there.

On the other side of the train stood the Hitler Youth bugle band playing lively marches for the 16-year-olds who were saying good-bye to their mothers. These young boys had to leave for the front to fight and were hanging on to their mothers and crying. Well, I had my three days on the train and had a lot to tell mom and Al. Sometimes mom, Al, and I would take a train into Kulmsee, situated on a lovely, large lake, just 12 miles away. I also made trips to Bromberg, Graudenz, and Marienwerde.

In the meantime, Mr. Krentz and his beautiful horse were drafted into the Army, but he had to march while an Army officer rode his horse.

Aunt Minna now lived in Posen, in Polish the town is called Posnan. Mom and Al went to visit Aunt Minna. That's where they met Cousin Theo Savins' fiancée Susie. She was born in Schwetz, across the Weichsel from Kulm. She was Polish but spoke German very well. Susie's younger brother had been killed by the Germans. She admitted to Al that her brother must have belonged to the Polish resistance while in Posen.

Susie owned several pairs of real nice ice skates and she let us know that if we wanted them we would have to pick them up. So, a short time later, Al and I took the train to Kulm. From Kulm we crossed the Weichsel River on foot. We had to walk approximately four miles on ice. There was no bridge. Susie gave us the skates plus a pinball machine with bells on it. Now we really had something nice. Al and I walked back to Kulm that evening. We were getting mighty hungry by now, after all that walking on ice.

In Kulm we found a nice "Hotel Deutsches Haus." It smelled good in there. Even though we had money and ration cards, all one could get was spinach. It was steamed and tasted just like it looked—wartime food. That's all that was available to us since we did not have enough points on the ration cards. While we were waiting, we set up our little pinball machine. We really went to work on that: the bells were ringing, the ball was bouncing, but not for long. The tall waiter in his black suit was soon standing over us.

With his fish-mouth face he said, "You quit playing or you leave." We quit playing.

When Al and I returned from Kulm, a pleasant surprise awaited us. Dad was home. He was as happy as we were. There were lots of hugs and all four of us were talking at the same time. Dad stayed with us for a whole week. I introduced him to my Polish friends. We had a lot of laughs and good food thanks to Mrs. Krentz.

Dad was concerned about Johann and so were we. Johann was born in 1929 so he would be 16 in July of 1945. Dad, however, felt that the war might not last that long. The German generals had tried to blow up the Paper Hanger, but he came out alive— this time even nuttier than before. He had over 2,000 officers killed who knew about the attempt. So now, with the greenhorns running things, the war might only last another six months. So Johann might not have to go at all.

"As for myself," said dad, "I drive my wagon loaded with bread to the front lines. I keep my head low and no bullets can go through the bread."

Before dad left, he took Al and me aside and told us, "If the Russians come close, take mom and leave for the West, we'll meet up there somehow when all this is finished."

Mom walked dad to the railroad station alone. When she came back we just sat in our room all gloomy, no one talked. We were all afraid we would never see him again.

Al and I planned a trip to Kulm for the following Saturday morning to see Aunt Wanda and cousin Gerhard. Ruth was still with the Red Cross and our other cousin, Irmgard, was in the same school as John, in Hela by the Baltic Sea. Their other brother, Ewald, was on the Russian front somewhere in Lithuania or perhaps back in East Prussia.

So at 6 a.m. we left for the railroad station. It was dark and foggy. Daylight there came at about 8:30 a.m. We had to pass a cemetery; it had tall, dark hemlock trees all around and looked very spooky. One bright morning in the summer, as we had walked by the cemetery, we saw an old man dangling from a tree. Who knows why he hung himself and why at the cemetery? Was it because few people walk by there at night? We reported this at the railway station.

So now, in the dark at six in the morning, we talked extra loudly to hide our fear as we walked by. Living people did not scare us, we could outrun them. But this dark, mysterious place could be full of demons. Al was 13 and I was 12 years old. This was not our home. This was unfriendly and strange West Prussia, and it was so divided—German, Polish, back and forth.

Well, we made it past the cemetery, and now there were just the thick Basswood trees without leaves and in the distance, about a mile away, the lights of the station. Suddenly a dark shadow leaped out from behind a tree and landed right in front of us. We just about died of shock. Then he, our brother Johann, laughed at us. What a bad joke. He said he'd heard us talking in the quiet of the night from a quarter mile away. All three of us walked back, this time paying no attention to the cemetery. After all, we were three again, a full army unit, what was there to fear?

Johann had just gotten off the night train going south. He had a few days off and wanted to see us and pick up an extra blanket and some more warm clothes, mainly underwear. He said that school now looked more like a paramilitary academy with all the students wearing the Hitler Youth uniforms to class. He could not quit going there even if he wanted to. He had to sign back in on a certain date. Mom and dad had no say about that. Johann had to be where the dictatorship told him to be.

One sunny, frosty winter afternoon Al and I were skating on the farm pond when two young boys in Hitler Youth uniforms showed up on the ice. They had a message for us—more like an order. We were to attend the Hitler Youth meetings on Sunday mornings or there would be penalties. We were not worried since we'd gotten away with not going back in Lithuania and now what could they do to us? Now, that the Russians were coming?

By now it was late November. Mr. Plit had to go into the Army also. He had taken on German citizenship about five years previously and was "eingedeutscht" and had to serve. Now Mr. Orlowski was put in charge of the horses. Al and I would sneak in some extra quarts of oats for the horses daily. Boy did those horses look good and were they ever full of energy!

At evening time, coming off the farm and walking on the open road, Al and I could see the rockets going up in the clear sky. Those must have been aimed at Britain. They were likely the dreaded terror weapon the V-2's sent from Pinemunde by the Baltic Sea. We wondered if Johann and dad could see them also or were they too far away?

Suddenly there was no more school. By now Al and I had possibly had four months of schooling that year. That's more than the previous year in Lithuania. And just when I'd gotten used to writing in the modern Latin alphabet! I did not care much for the Gothic letters and Roman numerals anyway.

One night Mrs. Krentz asked me to walk with her to our neighbor Nannt. It was pitch-dark. Halfway there we saw a man walking toward us.

Mrs. Krentz whispered to me, "If he asks us anything, we'll speak to him in Polish." Will you look at that! Now that the tide was turning, she could all of a sudden speak Polish! But when I was running with the Polish lads, she and Mr. Krentz would frown at me. As it was, the young man just walked by us, and we looked straight ahead and kept going. When we got there I did not go into the house. I told her I'd wait outside. I had my reasons.

Some time ago, during the summer, I was here checking out the pond. I knew Nannt's softy son, so I asked him if there were any fish in this pond. He did not know, no one had ever fished in it. Well, I had quickly found a wire mesh basket, about a six gallon size, stuck a seven foot hay-fork handle through it, tied it on, and started dragging it Lithuanian-style through the pond. Wow, there were plenty of Karossen, the fish with pink and yellow fins. When I got a mess of them, I had put them on a stick and walked home with them. Stevka, the Polish cook, had made a beautiful meal out of them for all of us.

So, a week later I went back to the pond to do some more fishing. Not this time, though. Mr. Nannt, it seems, was already waiting for me.

He started hollering, "Wer hat dir's geheissen?" (Who gave you permission to fish here?) Just from the few words he spoke I knew he did not know High German or East Prussian. He was a Schwab, notorious for being tight. He would make a Scotsman look like a big spender. I quickly turned and headed back across the fields.

After about a half hour, Mrs. Krentz came out of the house and we headed back to her farm. She was sad and serious and said to me, "It looks like we'll have to run also, we'd better get our gear in order, wagons and horses."

At the farm she asked my mother if she would like to go by train with us boys, or with her (Mrs. Krentz) and her wagons. Mom said she'd discuss it with Al and me. We thought about it for a day. The trains were very unreliable and they were daily targets of low-flying planes. Sometimes they were side-railed and one could freeze to death in them. And lastly, when the rush came, you had a hard time getting on them as people became vicious. One could only stand for so long on the steps of a moving train before you started to freeze, fall asleep, and fall off. Hypothermia could hit anytime.

Al and I liked the horses. My dream was to travel like a gypsy and see all the lands and people. So far though, we had no permission to leave. So Mrs. Krentz and I went to the Ortsgruppenführer, a very important sounding name for a mouthpiece and messenger boy for the Reich. He told us that no one was to leave now, but maybe by mid or late January.

Christmas came. Mom, Al, and I sat in our room wondering about Johann and dad. We had no radio. We just stayed in place. The New Year came and we were still there. Mrs. Krentz always had nice food and Al and I would wash up, comb our hair, and sit up straight to enjoy it. Mrs. Krentz liked that.

CHAPTER 9

By January of 1945 the stirrings of the approaching war could be felt. There were many more army personnel around setting up communication lines. Army traffic moved by day and night, but this was nothing new to us. We were used to it.

We had to get ready to move on again. This would be our sixth move since 1939. The bad part was that we did not know where we would go, or how would we live? How could dad and Johann find us? The uncertainty was creepy. On the other hand, we knew we should be going west since the Russians might get here in the middle of the night with a big band of tanks, cannons, troops, and rapists. Then we would be doomed. If we weren't killed, we could be sent to Siberia and live under the Communist boot.

In mid January, Mr. Orlowski prepared the big field wagon with a top made of thin willow branches. Big blankets and tablecloths were tied over them. Slowly Mrs. Krentz had that big wagon loaded with bedding, a dresser, and her nice Persian carpets. Mom was to sit in the middle of the wagon with Traut-Marlen, Mrs. Krentz's six month old baby girl. Al was to be up front with Mrs. Krentz, as she intended to drive the two-horse team: the left one named Hans and the right one Bonnek. These two were not the real heavy plow horses, but were good for pulling wagons on the road—usually loaded with potatoes and sugar beets—to the railroad terminals. They looked lively and beautiful with their black shiny legs and chestnut colored bodies.

The smaller "Ackerwagen" had wooden spokes and wheels with a 1 ½-inch band of metal around them. This wagon's body was of 1 ¼-inch wood; it was a heavy, sturdy wagon. I was to ride in it with Frieda.

Mrs. Krentz never asked me to drive the wagon; she must have considered me too young. She designated Frieda as the driver. When I heard this, I spoke up for the first time ever and told her that I would drive since Frieda had no experience with horses other than knowing that oats go into the front end and come out in the rear. She was a nice, delicate city girl stuck on the farm. I let Frieda sit next to me. This was my wagon now, my responsibility: the people, the horses, and the wheels.

My wagon was the same as Al's only a little lighter and smaller with two guide bars, one on each side of the horse. We loaded this wagon with burlap bags full of oats to take us to the farthest west of Germany. We also had a wood saw, hammer and nails, grease for the axles, and spare chains that the horses used to pull the wagons.

My horse's name was Lulu and he was poetry in motion. He was bigger and heavier than a Belgian, but not quite as heavy as a Clydesdale. He was pinkish with an off-white tail and mane. The long hair over his hooves looked like heavy boots. He walked with a slow stride and when he slammed his hooves down the ground shook ever so slightly. I can only guess his weight at 1,400 to 1,800 lbs.

Al's horses, Hans and Bonnek, were smaller and faster. We fed our horses extra rations of oats for the last six weeks just to see them get spunky. Lulu's hinder was as wide as a table. Mr. Orlowski said jokingly, "Four guys could play a game of blackjack comfortably on that rear end."

All three horses had new shoes with ¾-inch high H-cleats turned into them. We also stashed more of these on the wagons along with a wrench. By now there were many retreating German soldiers arriving on the farm and staying in the barn to keep warm. Mrs. Krentz kept busy cooking for them. This left Al and me with the freedom to put what we liked onto the wagons. We also tied bicycles to the back of the wagon. Al and I had never owned any.

I had snuck into the basement and found a full 15-gallon glass wine bottle in a woven reed basket which it took the two of us to carry. At the top of the bottle lay a siphoning hose. I tried the contents which were sweet and tangy. We added the bottle to the wagon between the oat bags.

My wagon had one willow-branch bow over the driver's seat and we draped a blanket over it and that cut down the cold winter wind on our necks. Al's wagon was covered front to back.

CHAPTER 10

It was January 1945 and on the morning of 28th, we finally set out. I will never forget the date. Mr. Orlowski had hitched the horses. Mom went into Al's front wagon under the cover. Mrs. Krentz brought out Traut-Marlen, the 6 month old baby, gave her to mom and sat down next to Al who was holding the reins. The horses could not wait any longer; they were anxious to finally move. I drove the back wagon with Frieda sitting next to me.

We drove by my friends' house that waved and wished us well. "Go with God, Jushu," they called. As the first wagon went by they stayed in the house, but they came out when I rode by. Mrs. Krentz sat stiffly, looking straight ahead, not a tear in her eyes. I, on the other hand, was happy to be underway, I just wanted to keep moving. But it was cold. It must have been near zero degrees. The wheel axles on the wagons squealed like stuck pigs. The ancient cobblestone road was quite uneven and covered, like the fields, with a foot of snow. Ice formed around the horses' mouths and whiskers. The ice on the road presented no trouble to Lulu. When he planted his cleats down, his hooves always hit the stone or dirt. All I had to do was keep the wagon in the center of the road so it would not slide to either side. There was no traffic going east as far as the eye could see.

Two farmers and their families joined our wagon train. They were in their late thirties or early forties. There was nothing physically wrong with them that I could see, yet they were civilians. They must have had some reason for not being in the service. Their names were Strobel and Kilper, and they had small children with them. Al decided to let their wagons lead. We drove like that for most of the day, non-stop.

Something loomed up ahead. The whole train of wagons stopped. I wanted to see what the hold-up was and told Frieda to stay put. I could make out some kind of hill a few miles ahead but it was getting dark. We continued on in stop-and-go traffic. Finally, we neared the hill, which turned out to be a dike for the Weichsel River and we were on the lowlands alongside it. That's why we hadn't seen any villages during the past few hours.

We had to cross the Weichsel on ice, but first had to get over the dike. There was a trail made for the farmers. In the summer they led their cows and the hay wagons over. But now it was sheer ice. Al and I appraised the situation and we decided that it would be no problem for our horses. The ice was solid and the cleats would hold. One by one the farmers went up to the dike and disappeared out of sight on the other side. Stobel went, then Kilpert, and now it was our turn. Our hearts were pounding with anticipation.

Just then a loud and excited farmer from behind us yelled, "What are these kids doing on the wagons?"

He thought we might be holding up the trek of wagons behind us, since he did not see an adult driver. We heard the thunder of bombs or cannons in the distance, and were surprised that the front lines were so near when we saw the sky lit up. We all wanted to get across as fast as possible but the right way to proceed was one at a time. If one wagon stopped at the top, the ones behind would slide backwards and end up in a big pile of people, horses, and wagons.

Well, this guy had a horsewhip and ran up to Al's team and, in his craze and panic, whipped Hans and Bonnek. They leaped forward and one broke a chain. The wagon stood still. We were still on level ground. That's when I lost it for the first time in my life. I pulled out dad's double barrel shotgun that was rolled up in a blanket. I jumped off my wagon, screamed at him waving my gun with one hand and wiping away tears with the other. This could just as well have been the end of our run. If all was ruined, if the harness was broken, and if the distant bombs hit us, it would be his cruel act that had caused it.

"If you touch these horses again," I yelled, "You'll be dead."

He took off as fast as he arrived but still had to snarl, "There should be a law against kids having guns. I will report you."

I quickly hid my gun again. Al said that only two chains were busted and within a few minutes we had our spare chains out and in place. Al almost had to hold those two excited horses back as he went across the dike. I cannot tell you how proud I was of Al. He was leaning forward across his wagon gate, his arms stretched out, holding the reins tightly, talking encouragingly to his horses. He had good control of them. Al was a much milder character than I, not quite as daring, but look at him now!

Lulu, my gelding, was stomping nervously, wanting to be with the other two horses, his pals. So I just released his rein and tapped him lightly with it. He sprang into action instantly. When we hit the hill and the load slowed him down, he lowered himself like a lion on the prowl. He made short, forceful steps, had his tail slightly raised, and I could see folds forming on his thighs. The minute we got to the top I slowed him down. Al was descending slowly and I had to take in the picture of the landscape.

To the left were three or four wagons that had rolled off the dike. Some farmers had put 2x4s or other boards through the spokes and stopped the wheels from turning. The wagons had become sleds and slid sideways off the trail, rolling down the embankment. I saw people milling around on the bottom, gathering their spilled belongings. I was sure some of them were hurt but there was no stopping.

Now I started my downhill ride. I knew Lulu could hold us back. He held his front legs stiff and straight and his hind legs real low, his big hinder almost on my seat. I was telling him what a nice guy he was. We made it down just fine, slowly and without slipping. Frieda was praying quietly. I knew now that Lulu really listened to me and we were a team. We would be seeing the west together—unless we were shot before we got there. The way Lulu lowered his head and body and sped up the hill with hot steam coming out of his nose, he resembled a locomotive. I was so proud of him and that picture is etched in my mind.

On the bottom of the dike it was flat again. We did not know where the meadow ended and the water began. It was all ice and snow and we just kept moving toward the west shore as I could now determine that we were on the river. The trail was marked by some Christmas trees stuck in the ice. There were also some holes in the ice where some bombs had hit. Suitcases and pillows were floating in the waterholes where wagons had sunk. By morning the holes would be frozen again like a lid on a coffin. That was the end of another family's history.

I kept holding Lulu back, he always wanted to be right behind Al's wagon but that would be too much weight on one spot. I surely did not want to sink. The thought of that scared me more than the bombs going off on the not-so-distant shore.

The other shore did not have a dike but had a slow steady rise. We had no trouble moving on for the next few hours and even saw some villages. All of us were tired now. The countryside was silent. No bombs, no explosions.

Al steered us through one village at the end of which was a nice, abandoned farm. We pulled into the yard and unhitched the horses. There was plenty of room in the warm barn. Al and I started hauling water from the pump outside for the horses. My, were they thirsty! There was also hay and we gave them their ration of oats. Then we went to the farmhouse. Mrs. Krentz already had some warm food for us and did it ever taste good! It had now been fifteen hours since we left Mrs. Krentz's farm but to us it seemed like days. We hurried back to the barn and buried ourselves in the nice warm hay. We kept our clothes and shoes on and fell asleep in minutes after such a long first day.

Mom shook us when it seemed we had just closed our eyes, "Wake up, wake up." She looked worried as she held our barn lantern in her hand and did not leave.

She said "Listen, explosions." Sure enough, we could hear some in the vicinity. Al and I gave the horses water. It looked like they had been eating all night. We put on their harnesses. Lulu's slipped easily over his head, and I cinched the bottom strap. But when I put the bridle over his head behind his ears, I could tell he did not want that cold iron bit in his mouth. He lifted his head way up high with me dangling on the bridle way up there. I could almost see him grinning and making sport of me. I hung on until he lowered his head and told him harshly that he had better listen, which he did. Now I was ready to go with him to the yard where the wagon was standing.

When we came close to the three foot gate in the fence, he stopped. I could not persuade him to go through the gate. Al was already hitching one horse to the wagon and mom held the other. But here I was with Lulu refusing to go through the narrow gate. I gave up the pulling contest, he had me stymied there. So I walked him in a circle and then started to back him up as if hitching him to the wagon. He went through the gate backwards just like that. I quickly hitched him to my wagon and off we went. Mom had made me a sandwich, which tasted really good on this dark frosty morning.

Again we drove all day with the bombing gradually becoming less audible. We kept going west—whenever the Army let us move forward—for the next eleven days. If there was an Army unit or convoy going west, we had to pull into the ditch and sit there for hours to let them by. But everything was becoming pretty much routine now for Al and myself. We would hunt for hay and oats for the horses and keep ours in reserve—and we just kept on driving.

The weather was at least ten degrees warmer now and there were long stretches of road with no ice. On one sunny day we arrived at a nice village by a long lake. The ice on the lake glistened in the sun. Both we and the horses were pretty tired.

We chose a neat, abandoned farm and stayed for at least three days. Al and I slept in the house and in the morning mom had a pan of warm water for us to wash our faces. I would strip down to the waist and lean over the pan as I splashed the water over my face, rub it quickly, and blow the air loudly out of my mouth. That's how our farm helpers did it in Lithuania. When I dried my face I saw the other people who were staying there snicker. After that, I washed quietly and not when there were strangers about. At twelve years of age, I figured I was as good as any man and did not need to be laughed at.

It was a good place to stay and added a little bit of normalcy to our escape. It did not last long. The village started to fill up with other people from the east and with Army units. So on a bright morning we left this once-quiet village.

The "Kettenhunde," military police, were out on the highway. They would stop any wagon at will and look for men ages 16 to 54. If they found someone, the person would have to produce documentation proving their exemption from the armed services. These military "chain dogs" always scared me. They neither smiled nor spoke nicely. They wore steel helmets and long, heavy, green overcoats with black, shiny high-shaft boots. Over the coat they buckled a black belt and a pistol sidearm. Around their neck they wore a heavy chain with 1 inch links from which hung a large metal plate, approximately 3" x 10" long. It looked like silver, but I bet it wasn't.

They looked into Mr. Kilper's wagon and barked "Papiere" (papers). They talked to him a while about "Volkssturm" possibly further down the road. It was a type of "civil service" for old and young civilians allowing them to be assigned into the army as needed. The Paper Hanger was running out of soldiers since they had been captured or killed in Africa, Greece, Yugoslavia, in the Baltic countries, but mainly in Russia. Many regular Army soldiers who were fighting in the west now volunteered to go to the eastern (Russian) front to keep the Russians out of Germany. They volunteered by the thousands and died by the thousands.

Anyway, these military policemen came mainly from the cities where most of them had worked for some law-enforcement organization. Those cities were now about eighty-nine percent flattened. Their wives and children were sent to towns and villages. The wives worked in shops producing something for the war effort. Working right next to the wives in the shops were the French war prisoners. Some made friends and some became pregnant by the good-looking young Frenchmen. That would make any German front-line soldier very unhappy.

Now the MP looked into my wagon. He had a large belt buckle about 2 ½" x 3" with an eagle sitting on a swastika and around that emblem it read "Gott mit uns" (God with us). It looked to me like this MP never prayed, but he did wave us on.

We kept going to wherever they let us go, so one nice, sunny afternoon we came into a town called Buetow in Pommern—Pomerania—the real Germany, not West Prussia anymore. I had no map and had only once seen one in Lithuania, so I did not know how far west we had come. Mr. Kilper knew that instead of going straight west, we were led more north towards the Baltic Sea. So now we kept going in a westerly direction whenever possible.

The unimportant country roads were not as crowded and there was less danger of being strafed by low flying fighter planes. We traveled westward for possibly 10 days. Before we knew it, we were approaching Koeslin (in Pomerania). But Koeslin was being bombed so we steered southwest of that city.

Traveling now did not seem such a hardship. I was always happy when we were moving toward the west. I could imagine the nice places that my dad had told me about in the Rhineland. On weekends he and his brother Albert would take a boat to a town called Kettwig-Werder, not far from Essen. It was beautiful there, I was told. That description stayed with me. I could take

43

anything here on the long road, as long as I got where I wanted to be and where dad told us we would meet.

Kolberg now lay ahead of us. That city was right on the Baltic Sea. We had to proceed more southward and stay away from the coastal area. If the Russians made a fast push to the west, they would have us in their trap. To get out alive by ship was almost impossible.

The news had reported that the "Wilhelm Gustloff" was sunk with approximately 5,000 refugees. About 1/5 of them were saved. Shortly before, as the Russians made a fast push out of East Prussia, the "Goya," which was overloaded with 7,000 people aboard, sank as it was torpedoed and only 200 were saved. My friend, Manfred Nitschmann, was one of the people cut off by the Russian army. His whole family waited in line for a few days on the docks during the time the ships were sunk. But that did not discourage them. They went out on the next ship and made it to Danzig alive. Al and I were sure we would not be going on any ship or ferries. All we had to do was stay far ahead of the Russians.

Now we had to leave Kolberg and travel almost due south for about 160 miles, but traveling became much more difficult. When we came into Greifenberg, this beautiful town was filled with a lot of Army troops, artillery, tanks, and trucks. I found out why. There were no bridges north of Stettin on which to cross the Oder River. Maybe the ferries were overloaded or bombed and there was no more ice on the Oder, so everybody was going southwest now.

The town square in the center of the city of Greifenberg seemed like a good spot to stay overnight. Al and I hated sleeping in schoolhouses or dancehalls. The straw in there smelled bad and it was populated with lice. Kids were crying all night and old folks would cough without end. We would rather be chilly and freeze a little bit but have peace and quiet on our rigs. In this crowded town, we kept one eye on our horses. People would steal and eat them and others might need a horse to go west. We watered them and tied them to our wagon. I could hear Lulu's loud chomping, he had a good appetite. Once in a while he would stomp his hoof, but to me it sounded like music. Mom, Frieda, Mrs. Krentz, and the baby always slept in the houses.

Frieda was talking to some soldiers who told her she was crazy to stay with Mrs. Krentz. She should instead look for her parents. My opinion was that she should have gone home before we left Mrs. Krentz's farm. I don't know if she was afraid of government retaliation for not fulfilling her one year obligation, or if she was afraid to travel the 18 km (11 mi) to Culmsee alone. Anyway, within a few minutes she had her suitcase in her hand and walked over to a military truck where there were many hands to help her up. At 17 years old, the blond, slender girl would be well taken care of by the soldiers. That was the last time I saw or heard from Frieda. She could not handle horses, but she prayed nicely and I liked that in this harsh, heartless world.

Now it was nighttime in Greifenberg. There were no bombs and Al and I sat back under our carpet roof. I stuck the rubber hose into our big wine bottle and we both took some hearty swigs of that good-tasting wine. We sat back and listened to the bells in the bell tower playing lovely melodies. Man, was that good! I could take that any day. We were on the move! I was feeling good!

Chapter 11

At sunup we told Mrs. Krentz that Frieda was gone and she just nodded. We were heading for Naugard, another old beautiful city. The roads were really congested and the warplanes were swooping over us. We gave them plenty of targets to shoot at.

I looked to my left. There were two low-flying planes making a run toward us. Al saw them too. He was going to jump off the wagon with Traut-Marlen, who was now seven months old, but I was already there next to his wagon. He quickly tossed her down to me lightly and I caught her. She was giggling. To her this was fun. We all hit the ditch together and lay there for a few seconds until the burst of gunfire was over. I gave her back to Al who handed her to her mom and the wagons rolled on. Not one of us was hit.

One morning, while we were in Gollnau, I got word that there were oats to be had at the other end of town. I quickly hitched Lulu and went to get some. Meanwhile, Al would hitch his horses and help load the women and baby, and by then I should be back. I got to the elevator, picked up my oats, and was happily trotting back when, all of a sudden, while at a crossroad, a fighter plane – engine whining like a siren – flew right down on me. He came in a steep dive and then fired. The shots that hit the cobblestones were terribly loud. I was crouched on the floor of the wagon with my face in the straw, and the bullets hit the front gate where my feet usually were.

I was so shocked and mad that the hair on my neck stood up like on a mad dog! Here I was, I made friends with everyone, in every place and country like Lithuania, Poland, Russia, Prussia, and Germany, and I treated everybody I knew nicely (except maybe that Swabian-German who hit our horses on the dike; if we could not have fixed our gear before the Russians arrived, I might have shot him if I'd seen him again). But here I was, as nice as could be, and a plane finds it necessary to dive at me, shoot, and singe the hair on the top of my head. Lulu was injured on his hind leg, on the bottom near his hoof where the meat is tender, and he was limping a little, but we were moving.

This end of town was deserted. People must have left here the previous day. There was a nice new bicycle lying on the side of the street. I stopped and threw the bike on top of the oats and went to tell Al how really, really mad I was that they shot specifically at me. Al was happy to see me back and we put some carboleneum (tar-like substance) on Lulu's back hoof. He did not like it. It must have burned or hurt him and he stomped his hoof madly but not hard because that would hurt even more. Then I showed Al my newly-found bike. Wow, was he happy! We now had a bike of our own! But that happy moment did not last more than five minutes. Mrs. Krentz came out and the first thing she said was, "What is that bike doing on that wagon?"

"I found it, it's mine," I said.

"Throw it off right now," she shrieked, "you have two bikes already." So, with a heavy heart, I threw the bike off the wagon.

The next day, after we stopped for the night, I tested Mrs. Krentz. I untied her husband's bike from the wagon without asking her and rode off with it to town to look around. It was a small town. Another twelve-year-old boy smiled at me when he caught up to me. I asked him if he lived here and he said no. They were also moving with the wagon train. But his dad and mom were with him and he was allowed to check things out by riding his bike.

"Wow," I said, "You are lucky to have your dad with you and have fun checking things out. Don't forget to jump in the ditch when danger comes."

We rode our bikes back and parted. I tied up Mr. Krentz's bike and Mrs. Krentz never said a word. Of course, she was dependent on me and Al. If we took off with the train or caught an Army truck, what could she do with that baby? So she never gave us a bad time except that I was still miffed about being shot at and having to throw away that beautiful bike. It snowed lightly overnight, but it quickly melted and ran down the wide highway once we resumed traveling.

We could see the fighter planes swooping down far ahead of us so, for the time being, we had nothing to worry about. The sun was warming me now, the snow was melting, and soon it would be spring and warm. I sat back in my wagon and told Lulu how nice it would be for him once the meadows greened up. I ran up to Al's wagon and asked if I could have a sandwich. Mrs. Krentz always made good ones. She must have prepared a lot of hard salami back at the farm because she had a plentiful supply of it.

We eventually came up to the hill where we had seen the planes doing their deadly work. They would fly above the wagon trains and shoot at them. Sometimes the target was an Army convoy, but mostly it was us kids, babies, mamas, and grandparents. In this all-out war, no one was sorting things out. You just flew your plane and shot at anything that moved. There were 17 million people from the east who made it to the west, but millions never did.

We arrived at the hill where the planes had earlier been strafing just as I was eating my tasty sandwich. Then things got ugly. We came up to a beautiful Belgian horse lying in shock; it had been shot and was shaking, emitting a quiet squeal. Up came a group of French war prisoners, guarded by a German soldier. These guys did not have a good salami sandwich, they were starving.

They ran to the shaking horse, the soldier shot, and the prisoners instantly started cutting up the horse. The blood was running down the hill along with the melting snow. I could not finish my sandwich. I felt so sorry for that beautiful horse with the golden mane. I threw away the rest of my sandwich and unfortunately threw up what I had already eaten.

However, Al and I were on a mission. We were going to deliver our loads and show the world that we did it. So I never once complained to mom that I was tired or sick of this traveling or being shot at—never. Al and I looked at this trip as an adventure. Wait until we told dad and Johann what we'd been through! I straightened myself up, wiped my face and tears, took a deep breath and gazed at Lulu walking steady as a rock, marching down the highway, looking straight ahead and not at the bloody snow.

But as we went on further, we came across men digging a hole with women standing around watching. The sandy hillside was not frozen so they made good progress with their digging. All of a sudden I saw a boy's bike lying in the ditch. The smiling boy from yesterday was under a blanket, dead. He was lucky to have had his dad with him, but that did not protect him from the plane's bullets. I did not cry, but I was very sad as I pulled the wagon back onto the road. Lulu was anxious to catch up to Al's team. Again, I focused straight ahead and at Lulu. Man, it was great to be alive! Outwardly, I looked fine, but on the inside my heart was pounding and I trembled slightly. Nonetheless, I controlled myself. This was a dangerous highway indeed!

Mr. Strobel and Mr. Kilper suggested we use some side roads so we drove off this Autobahn (highway) and went through some small villages, somewhere between Stettin and Stargard. It was nice and quiet there. That night we found an abandoned farm, cleaned ourselves up, changed clothing, and supplied our horses with fresh hay. The next morning we hitched our horses, but Strobel and Kilper did not. They and their wives decided they would not die crossing the Oder River. They would rather stay alive and work for the Russians. Mr. Kilper and I were almost like father and son. I listened and learned a lot from him.

He said, "Josef, it will only get worse and if you make it across the two bridges you might get killed by the bombers. They drop 1,000 tons per day and sometimes more. Look how nice and peaceful it is here in the countryside."

I just shook my head. Al and I looked at one another with a grin. We went out and hitched the horses without asking mom or Mrs. Krentz what they wanted to do. If they had wanted to stay, I think Al and I would have run across the bridges on foot. But we saw the women hug each other and saying their good-byes, so we knew they were coming with us.

In order to cross the Oder River, we had to get back to the Autobahn. It was easy traveling now. All four lanes across were open to the west. No one was going east, so the highway was not crowded. Once on it, one could not get off until one was on the other side of the river. We were on some flatlands or marshes without exits. We stopped the horses on the side of the expressway and fed them. It looked like it would take all night to get to the bridges. Just before dark we came close. We were hoping that the attacks would halt at dark. There was some action around the bridges. I saw some small planes occasionally buzzing around the first bridge, but I did not see whose planes they were and, besides, we could not turn back now. There was no other way – no return.

As we approached some shot-up wagons, we saw about seven people covered with white bed sheets neatly laid out by the wayside. My mom asked me to look under the sheets to see if they were dad or Johann. I did not like to look at dead people, but I never said no to mom or dad. It took me only seconds to glance at them and then I ran back to my wagon with goose bumps on my body. "Not ours," I yelled.

Chapter 12

In the meantime it got totally dark. We were just about to get on the East Bridge when some fighter planes dropped off many bright and beautiful silvery-shining flares along the full lengths of both bridges. These flares were attached to very small parachutes, smaller than an umbrella. They illuminated the whole area around the bridges.

Then all hell broke loose!

The fighter planes came from behind, blasting us with cannon fire and dropping small bombs. Horses and people started running across the bridge. It sounded louder than a stampeding herd. The sound of the hundreds of steel-rimmed wheels, the thousands of hoofs, the bullets hitting the steel girders, but mainly it was those bombs, shattering the sound barrier. The children shrieked and the mommies pushing the baby buggies cried and screamed. To me it all seemed to occur in slow motion. Al was really moving ahead now; Lulu was flat-out galloping but losing distance to Al's two lighter and faster horses.

As we approached the middle of the bridge we were confronted with a "Panzersperre" (tank trap). The right lane was blocked by a 25 ft. high and 8 ft. thick fortress wall. All traffic had to cross to the left lane and then, just 10 ft. in, there was a wall in the left lane. One had to move to the right lane and again make a turn to the left, and then turn right once more to finally get through the trap. A tank could certainly not maneuver through such obstacles since it could not make such tight turns. Above the right lane of the bridge, was a suspended railroad car filled with concrete. The Army had intended to drop it into the middle of the trap just before the Russian tanks arrived.

So now all the traffic merged onto the left lane and some wagons passed me on the left. Lulu picked up more speed. He did not want to be separated from his buddies. Just then I saw Al make his right turn into the trap. He was leaning over his wagon gate, reins tight, arms stretched out and pulling hard to slow the horses. He knew he could not make the 180 degree turn inside the trap with that speed.

Now I came galloping into the trap. Hey, what's going on here? Some people ahead of me were not on their wagons and their horses started to back up. Were these people afraid to go through this bunker-type structure? Did they imagine it would prevent them from getting shot on the bridge? They were blocking my path!

I yelled at Lulu. He sped up along the center wall but the team ahead of me kept backing up and hitting me with the back of their wagon on my right side. Now I was pinned! But Lulu was not to be stopped. He went up in the air with his front body, lowered his hind legs, and then leapt. As he came down, his weight and back leg strength moved the other wagon sideways about four feet. He made three or four more such power hops and we had that other wagon pushed sideways out of the way. Once we were out of the trap we kept galloping down the bridge.

We almost caught up with Al who was in the right lane. I don't know if mom told him to slow down or if it was the heavy traffic, but when I came close to his wagon I heard mom cry out for me. I don't know what she said but I heard her voice. I hollered back, but just then a small bomb hit the bridge not far ahead of Al and her, so she did not hear me.

Al's horse Bonnek was taken down by the blast. Even I was hit with debris. Wagons, horses, and people were being thrown over the side of the bridge by the bomb blasts. Then, as I recovered from the blast, I picked myself off the floor of my wagon and I saw that Al was jumping off his wagon. He was intending to cut Bonnek's reins since the horse was lying on them. I knew the other horse, Hans, could pull that wagon off the bridge by himself. Just as Al leaned over Bonnek, the horse jumped up. He was alright! He had just been knocked down by the blast.

We then galloped a mile or so until we arrived at the so-called West Bridge. Here there was no trap, just a lot of screaming people calling out names. Everyone was running and looking for family members. The planes kept shooting and bombing. It sounded as though someone was playing a gruesome organ. We made it across the West Bridge without any incident and kept going at a high speed for a few more miles. It was nice and dark here without the planes. We could see the bridges behind us, lit up like the 4th of July with fireworks, but these explosions spread death to all the unfortunate people who happened to be on them.

Al finally stopped to rest the horses and to check up on me. I could not talk. That was a first for me since I love to talk. Not this time. I just took off my heavy winter coat and walked to the ditch. I really had to go and must have stayed there a half hour suffering with diarrhea. No one bothered me. Finally I pulled myself together and straightened up. I went to Al who was standing by his wagon waiting for me. The horses were steaming in the night air. We grinned at each other.

He said, "I thought we had it when that bomb hit ahead of us, but Bonnek is OK."

And then he laughed. "You should have seen Mrs. Krentz. You know that white dish pan we use for washing ourselves? She had it on her head and looked like a "Tommy" (British soldier), but it sure helped keep the gravel and dirt off her head."

We got back on our wagons and drove off the gruesome highway where we found a large abandoned farm, more like a mansion. Mom, Mrs. Krentz, and Traut-Marlen went in. Al and I unhitched the horses and gave them plenty of water, but they just nipped at the hay. I guess they felt abused too, in more ways than one. We had been on the road now for more than 22 hours. I was not hungry and neither was Al. We were in a nice, solid, brick barn. About 20 young calves were sleeping in their bins. We tied a rope across a corner of the bin, threw in some fresh straw, and dove into it. Wow, it was so nice and peaceful here. Within minutes we drifted off to sleep.

The next day we did not move. There were planes attacking the bridges. We knew the front line could be anywhere but not on this side of the Oder River. We knew that if the Russians made a surprise forward move, they could not cross the river that quickly, so we stayed on that big beautiful farm another day.

The horses got their appetite back and we rubbed them down and brushed them. By now, though, they must have lost some weight because we could more easily feel their ribs. As the farmyard filled up with Army trucks and soldiers, Al and I explored the mansion. We came across an enormously large room with 14 windows – what a waste. The room contained a Fluegel grand piano with a shiny, black, lacquered body. A young soldier was playing with vigor and intent, fast staccatos and then some mellow, smooth music. He must have been a concert pianist because he did not play any hit songs, monotone marches, or old polkas. After we completed our exploration, we again walked through the big room and saw the young soldier with his face in his hands, leaning forward silently. He may have been crying.

The next morning we hitched up the wagons and returned to the highway; we proceeded at a much slower pace since there was no need to hurry anymore. No one was shooting at us. We wondered if the bridges had collapsed, but there was plenty of traffic still heading west.

In a short while we encountered a Y in the road. The left lane headed for Berlin and the right lane headed to the west, toward Hamburg in northern Germany. There was a soldier standing where the highway split directing traffic. One half was to turn to the left and the other to the right: one wagon toward the southwest and the next to the northwest. His mouth was wide open and he believed himself to have more power than Napoleon. He wore a clean, green uniform, a shiny holster with a mean Luger, and polished boots.

An old farmer stopped his wagon next to the loudmouth soldier. The farmer knew us from the farm the night before. He asked the soldier to please direct the two wagons behind him to the west and his wagon toward Berlin. But the soldier just shouted louder and became more belligerent. His previous occupation was probably cleaning out manure for some farmer, but now he had power and the ability to command! He lifted his pistol and the farmer left in a hurry.

Al was leaning out of his wagon looking at me. I told him, in Lithuanian, to go ahead and I'd catch up in a minute. The soldier was barking at Al, "Los, los," (get going) and motioned him to the west. Lulu just followed him and the soldier became furious. He dropped his arms, looked at me, and motioned me toward Berlin. I had a hard time getting Lulu to go that way. He would take three steps and wait to turn around again. I had a very difficult time keeping him pointed toward Berlin.

I watched the soldier hollering at other families, and in the meantime he must have forgotten about me. I had a bunch of wagons following me now, but the left lane heading east was completely empty. I could feel the anger building up inside me. First, all the shouting and killing on the bridges and now, this loudmouth was trying to split us up! I am sure he was given instructions but he could have used discretion, not acted the way he did.

So I jerked Lulu's line to the left suddenly and he sprang to it instantly. He turned on that spot and within 10 steps he was already flying back eastward to the Y to make a turn to the west to follow Al's team. I held the reins tightly and slapped him with them as I approached the fork, made my left turn directly between two wagons, and then steered Lulu ahead toward the loudmouth. With only seconds to spare, he realized that the horse was heading straight for him. The soldier jumped into the ditch as we flew past him. I was ducking down between the gate and seat. It did not take long to catch up to Al's team as all the wagons I passed were moving at walking speed. I was not afraid of the loudmouth. He had no transportation and would have to wait for his relief at the post and besides, "my horse must have shied."

I was surprised at myself. I was never this violent in my life. I guess it was the dictatorial manner of the soldier and the thought of all the death going on around me that allowed me to act so daringly.

We continued our journey into the Mecklenburg area and then into Brandenburg province, traveling through pretty countryside. Most of the farms we encountered now were still occupied so we could not help ourselves to hay and oats, but there were hot soup stands set up in a few places, and life here seemed much more normal. On the other hand, no one here could advise us as to where to run. The allied forces were pretty close to us in the west. In fact, we heard through the grapevine that the American forces were already beyond the south of Berlin and heading east for Austria.

Al and I kept moving. We heard of the Elbe River, which was a couple hundred kilometers to the west and we definitely wanted to cross it. My Lulu was pretty tired by now. He had lost a lot of weight and a lot of his pep, but he continued to hold his head close to Al's wagon and just kept walking. By the time we arrived in the town called Neustrelitz, approximately in the center of the province of Mecklenburg, I felt so sorry for Lulu that I asked an old farmer what I could do for him. He suggested I feed him some boiled potatoes, but Lulu did not care for them. So the next day Al and I decided we would place Lulu in the lead. Oh, he did not like that at all. We had wanted him to be able to walk at his slower pace. Instead he would walk a mile and then stop to turn and look for Hans and Bonnek, his two buddies. He felt just fine again once we set him behind Al's wagon.

In my wagon there were two sticks nailed to the sides and tied at the top. We tied a woolen blanket to the sticks and pulled the blanket back a few feet on the bottom like a lean-to. With that added protection I was fine in those sub-zero January days and could take any cold weather—just like the horses. Al and I never caught a cold.

CHAPTER 13

The days passed, we kept moving, and soon it became March 1945. The sun was now able to warm us. No one had shot at us since the bridge crossing at the Oder River. On warm afternoons, I could even take off my heavy winter coat. Things were more regulated now. When we approached a town or village in the evening, some civilian would tell us where we could stay overnight and where to get something for the horses.

Lately, I'd seen Mrs. Krentz ask some villagers for directions but she never told Al or me why. Eventually, we approached the Elbe River and passed close to Festung Doemitz (the city of Doemitz). We looked for fighter planes but none came. We crossed the Elbe in bright daylight at a leisurely pace. Another eight miles west was the city of Dannenberg where we stayed the next evening. This was in the province of Niedersachsen or Lower Saxony, which borders Holland.

Mrs. Krentz finally let us know what her destination was. She had a sister living in Oldenstadt, right next to Uelzen. That's where her dad was living. We had always thought she was born in West Prussia. We quickly found out that the Germans from old Germany were not as talkative as the other decent German folks who were born abroad and had to get along with other nationalities.

The next day we pulled into Hohenzethen. There we came across a food station where an old man stood next to a kettle full of pea soup and a table with rye bread.

He poured a ladle full into each of our cups and then said, "I hope we don't have to put up with you people very long. Why didn't you stay where you came from?"

Mom broke out in tears. After all that scratching to get to the west, to find out that you were really unwanted, that hurt. But the next day we were on the road again and by late afternoon I looked up and read "Oldenstadt."

About twelve kids my age were walking alongside our wagons and reading our plaques on the sides. Each wagon had to have the farmer's name and address posted on the left side. Then one of them hollered, "That's my Aunt!" Mrs. Krentz had notified her sister that we were to arrive, and the kids were looking for us. I looked at the expressions on their faces. These kids had nice, clean clothes and clean milk-fed faces. Their moms called them in for three meals a day and they were a happy bunch.

My Lulu looked so down and was dragging himself along, his once-proud head now hung low. The deep groove in his hinder was gone. Instead he had the backbone showing from his mane to his tail and the hipbones were sticking out on the sides.

I was a sad picture myself. The heavy winter coat that had covered me in many cow barns, ditches, and on the wagon sorely needed cleaning and mending, and so did everything else that I was wearing. My lean-to blanket had holes from shrapnel, burns, and just plain tears from flying debris. We looked as we should after living for months just ahead of the front lines and sometimes right in the middle of them. Now we were in the middle of Germany, north of Berlin, and on the west side of the Elbe River. There was a glimmer of hope in me now. Maybe we'd made it, maybe this was it!!!

A couple boys jumped on my wagon, and one boy was on Al's. We made a right turn off Highway 191 into Oldenstadt, onto an old cobblestone street and up a slight hill. There were large, red brick houses and barns on both sides of the street. Then we crossed a little river that had a regular working grist mill with a river gate on its left side. A little further up was Meyer's Restaurant and guesthouse, and on the right was Kreb's Biergarten.

We continued up the hill and right in the middle, where the street split, were Schulz's six apartments and house. It had two stories and its red-brick walls were 18-inches thick. All north German houses had red-tiled roofs. It appeared we were on a small farm. There was a manure pile next to a barn in this small yard.

Al pulled up ahead of me, stopped his horses in the middle of the yard, and I pulled my rig up next to his. Our large farm wagons looked out of place here. As I found out the next day, they were not going to stay there very long. As I got off the wagon, Mrs. Krentz's sister greeted me in a friendly manner and she was the first person to give me a compliment.

She said, "You are so young and you drove this rig all across Poland and the provinces? We heard how many people died on the road and you made it."

No one else in northern Germany wanted to know how it went. They just took one look at me and knew I was an outsider, especially when I spoke. Here they spoke German with a very different dialect.

Mrs. Schulz agreed to give us one room. It had one window, one straight wall, and one slanted wall under the roof. We took our three suitcases off the wagons, up the stairs, and into the "Dachkammer" (attic room). Mrs. Krentz said she would set a table for us in her sister's kitchen. Al and I went to take care of our horses.

Mrs. Krentz said, "There is no need for that, the local farmers will take them."

She must have made these arrangements ahead of time. So that was it. Al and I watched Mr. Schutte lead off the three horses. Other people were now on the wagons, unloading them. Mr. Krentz's bicycle went to her nephew. Mom, Al, and I went up to that dark, lean-to room with the one window and sat on our suitcases. We did not know whether to be happy that we made it, or to cry for our pitiful situation. I knew I should have kept that bike from Prussia! Now I had nothing.

We had half a suitcase full of German money, but there was no housing to be had. Most of the cities were bombed out, so this was it, we stayed in Mrs. Schulz's house. She had a son my age, Willie Schulz. He had a brother, Herbert, who was about 7 years old.

Willie came into our room to ask if Al and I wanted to see the town. We became friends and checked out all the nooks and crannies of the village. Willie's dad had died in Russia a few years ago, so Willie was looking for friends. He was what I called a "milk face." Nice white skin, neat clothes, and one who never spent more than a couple hours outside in the cold.

He said he would like to hang with us, maybe because we looked hardened. He was right there! Al was of milder nature, but I would rather hit someone square in the face before I asked for a favor. My dad and his horses were delivering bread to the Germans at the Russian front lines. Now my Lulu was gone too. At this time in my life, I turned tough.

Mrs. Schulz liked Al and me and gave us a few pieces of clothing. When we walked in the village some bullies always picked on Willie and now, here he was standing next to his two friends.

One yelled, "Hey, Willie, where are you going with those two Pollacks?"

Al just grinned and walked past him. In Poland and Lithuania they called us Germans and here they called us Pollocks. Here we go again. Willie walked by the loudmouth and as I walked by him, he was about to make a move to either stand in my way or start a fight. He felt pretty strong with his two buddies next to him and he was a few years older and a bit bigger. I looked straight ahead but I could see him well on my left. I turned and hit him right in the pit of his stomach. As he bent forward he already felt my real quick left and right. As he stumbled backwards my leg tripped him and before he knew it, I had my knee on his chest. I did not hit him again. His two friends were 15 feet away by now and wanted no part of me.

Al said to me, "You're all red and shaking."

I answered, "I know, and if the other two had started something I could have finished them too." I was mad at everything.

When we got back to the house the wagons were gone too. Mrs. Krentz must have bartered them also. Nothing was said to Al and me. If we wanted to continue west we would have to walk. The railroads were almost totally shut down. Private and Army trucks were now running on fuel made of wood. Not many men were left here, most were scattered all over Europe and northern Africa. So, for now, Oldenstadt was it.

Willie Schulz had a girl cousin, also my age, named Ingrid Meyer whose dad had died in Russia. Ingrid had a little blond friend named Anne, whose house had been bombed in Hamburg. Ingrid and Anne lived in the same house now. Anne's dad was an engineer by trade who also died on the eastern front. So, Willie, Ingrid, and Anne were fatherless, but I knew that my dad was alive somewhere. We became fast friends and would walk the village. I ignored the bigger bullies because I knew I could not win against them but, I guess, I started to become a kid again.

Spring was coming now and it was getting warmer. The school house was filled with refugees from the east and so was every house in the village. The local authorities installed rows of chairs in the Kreb's dance hall to serve as classroom space. Al and I went there to register. You could not really call what we received as proper schooling. All ages sat together. It was more like a communal lecture class.

By now the front lines from the west were real close to us. When the sirens sounded, it took but fifteen minutes and the planes were on top of us. The Allies were already using the German airfields. The village bunker was built on top of the hill at the end of the village, so when the sirens sounded, school was over and everybody ran to the bunker or into their home basement.

One morning, Al and I did not go into the bunker. We did not want to sit there with the crying kids. Instead, we wanted to see if the planes were Mustangs, Spitfires, or Heinkels. There were so many places, walls, and brick stone fences to shelter behind that we felt perfectly safe outside. It was not like being on the expressway with no deep ditches available.

But the mamas complained to the teacher that we were in too much danger since the fighter planes took just minutes to arrive. So, school was again suspended.

The big bombers continued their flights over us by day and night. They came in bunches of 36, throughout the day, heading south toward Berlin and other big cities. All of them were four-propeller planes and they made the earth shake. They flew unopposed. Hitler must have run out of planes and fuel. He just sat in Berlin waiting for an end to his miserable life and to the end of the misery he had made Germany suffer.

God, this was a great time to be alive! There was so much going on every day. We did not know where to explore first. There was the city of Uelzen to explore with its population of 50,000. Lately, the bombers had flattened houses all along the railroad lines. The tracks were approximately three miles away from Oldenstadt. Al and I stood on Schulz's roof and watched the giant B 17's come across with flares and empty their racks of bombs in those squares of flares. The houses shook and the women yelled at us to get off the roof, but it was too exciting not to watch. Later on, however, the bombed out people came to our village and it got even more crowded in every house.

The 16-year-old boys and the men over 60 had to man the fire hoses. It took three boys to hold the "B" hose and they could only hold onto it for, at the most, 20 minutes. That hose walked them all over the place. The boys came home black with dirt and smoke and utterly exhausted.

Al and I and our new friend Willie were well off. There was no school and we were too young to be put into any service, so we went through the town exploring. I liked the city, the clean sidewalks, the white fences, the beautiful flowers, and the absence of mud, which had been everywhere on the last farm in Lithuania. At night, I would sit with Willie in their apartment and we would examine his atlas of the world—something I had never seen before. He also had a big map of Germany and there I saw another state called Nordrhein-Westfalen that went clear to the Rhine River and to Essen, where dad had worked when he was young. But we could not go there anymore because the Allied Forces had occupied it, and it would not be wise to go into another war zone especially since there was no need to go further.

Mom had to find a job in order to get food ration cards. Every able body had to have a job for the war effort and you needed a ration card to get anything. One night, after I fell asleep on my make-shift bed, a bomb went off at the edge of the village. I jumped up, about to hitch Lulu to the wagon and run, but then realized that there was no more Lulu for me and there was nowhere to run. So, whatever came our way, mom, Al, and I would have to fend for ourselves. I also prayed nightly for the safety of dad and my brother Johann and for them to find us.

During the day, Al and I would frequently go into the state forest, one mile south of the city, to enjoy the stillness and the soft breeze through the pine, beech, and oak trees and to hear the birds singing. I sorely wished for dad's horses so I could ride slowly through these woods without being shot at or bombed. I could dream. I knew that when I grew up I would drive a nice car like the doctor here in Oldenstadt, and I knew I would drive it all over the world.

Right now, though, I was very hungry; one could not get much with the ration cards, but we did get enough bread. If I helped Grandma Schulz rake hay for her two cows, she would make me a nice sandwich with ham or liverwurst. At night we would listen to Willie's mom's "Volksempfänger" (people's receiver) radio, a very simple plastic box that received only nearby stations and which had a cheap sound. It was a radio none the less. Hitler had promised every household a radio so that everyone could hear the propaganda and the monotone marches. In the evenings, after the news, there were some children stories and that was very interesting to me. This was at the end of March 1945.

The propaganda was much more subdued now in comparison to the camp in Nierenberg where we had stayed in 1941 and 1942. There was far less to brag about. At the camp the loudspeakers had spewed news of accomplishments every few minutes, such as how far into Russia our troops had advanced or how many ships they had sunk. Now, however, they could not announce that the Canadian and British armies were already close to us in Lower Saxony.

One morning, as the three of us boys were going to the forest on our regular stroll, we discovered an 88mm cannon by the edge of the woods in a low sandpit. It already had the camouflage net over it and some ammo stacked next to it. There was also a crew with a radio operator and guard. In a way we knew that the western front line was coming soon; what Al and I had heard through the grapevine was that the Russians were getting closer to the Elbe River also. But we guessed that the Allies would get here first. The wagons with the old men, moms, and kids were still arriving daily by the thousands. In Uelzen, the bombed out field was bulldozed, leveled, and a tent city was erected.

But still there was not enough room for all of the refugees. Some would overnight on the sidewalk and the following morning continue west or northwest to Bremen or Oldenburg, intent on getting away from the Russians. Then, one bright morning, it must have been in April, as I sat on the wooden chopping block in Schulz's yard, wham! A loud shot went right over our heads in a westerly direction. I almost fell off the block! Those 88s really were powerful. After about eight to ten rounds were fired, the church steeple in Uelzen was hit by the Allied Forces. The reason given was that the Germans had a spotter there. The steeple burned but not the church.

There was no German Army in my village of Oldenstadt, but one km south of the village the cannon was manned. As the steeple burned, a bunch of lighter bombers came over Uelzen and dropped bombs onto the business center in the middle of town. Later, it was said that the Allies told the German command to surrender the town or it would be bombed. Through the grapevine, we heard that the high-ranking commanders were at a big party at that time, in the Hotel "Stadt Hamburg," and did not want to leave to answer the Allies. The hotel did not get hit but a lot of civilians died that day.

The next day the Allies opened fire on Oldenstadt with their howitzers and tanks. Al and I ran to the basement. The rounds just got too close and were hitting everywhere.

The little basement was crowded with mamas, their children, and some grandparents. The barrage was coming closer now. One hit the big house where we lived. Mrs. Krentz's niece, who was about nine years old, started to scream. The next round hit directly over our heads. We knew the floors in these buildings were almost twelve inches of cement with steel bars. But when that one hit, I held my breath and wished I had gone deeper into the basement. The dust, gravel, and a heat wave came down the stairway and the girls screamed the loudest. I felt very uneasy and, truth be told, not so tough after being seared, but I did not scream.

People took towels, dipped them into buckets of water, and held them over their mouths and faces. Al and I had no towels, so we ran up the steps since the air in the basement was not breathable. The first thing we did outside was to pull the sandbags away from the windows. The minute that was done, the insiders opened them and the youngsters stopped screaming. They saw daylight and breathed. The barrage was over.

I looked around. The big house had been hit through the roof. Directly above us was a big hole in the tiled roof. I heard sizzling in the manure pile. Sure enough, there was a big piece of hot shrapnel laying there. The air had the familiar smell of explosives and as quickly as the barrage started it became quiet. I thought it had finished, but then it began again. Some brainless commander had the bridge blown up just below the village. Why blow up a bridge that was needed the next day for the British to enter the town? It was quickly repaired, being wooden, and only about 30 feet long.

The British came in open Jeeps without a shot being fired. Wow, we all ran out of our houses to watch the new arrivals. The older folks had to stay in the houses while the soldiers searched for weapons and German soldiers.

Then along came the mail carrier, a slightly heavy woman, who had a little knowledge of English, and who also lived in Schulz's house. She put on a nice blouse and lipstick, which was almost unheard of during the war in Germany, especially out in the country.

She stretched out her arms and walked toward the somber and stoic British soldier and said, "Hello, boys." He looked at her for a split second, lifted his hand as if to shake hers, but instead he took off her nice looking, gold wrist-watch and turned around and walked through the rest of the rooms.

The soldiers also collected all the cameras and gave "security" as the reason. In addition, they brought along pre-printed posters which they attached to all the houses in the village. These demanded all rifles and shotguns to be delivered to the front of the mayor's house by that evening. Anyone caught having a firearm after midnight would be shot. It also informed us that we were now governed by the "General Government" and we were to be off the streets by 7 p.m., after that we would be shot.

The women chased me around the house demanding to know where I had hidden my dad's beautifully carved double-barrel Austrian shotgun. I thought I might outrun them and they would give up, but they turned hysterical and I was going to get into real trouble with them unless I produce the shotgun. Heavy-hearted and thinking of dad – it was the only thing I had of his – I went to the woodshed and dug it up and brought it to the mayor's house. The soldiers stood there. They had smashed some of the old rifles, but the first soldier who saw my shotgun grabbed it from me. I walked away holding back my tears.

The next few days were very quiet. No electricity, no open stores, but a lot of occupation Army trucks rolling east. Then, slowly, the old men came out and started to fix up the buildings. I could hardly believe how fast and efficiently they worked. I also took a trowel of cement and filled some holes in the walls where the shrapnel had hit. Of course, I put my initials into the cement.

It took a few weeks to establish electrical service. The old guys really knew how to fix things. Now we could listen to any station we wanted and we were hungry for news. For the first time in our lives, Al and I tuned in to a US station and heard Glenn Miller's "In the Mood." Boy, did my heart race when I heard those happy tunes! There was new hope for me in this bombed-out world. There was Harry James with his trumpet sound and Gene Krupa's drum-beat. Something so new – so different! Man, this was a great time to be alive!

The first American trucks were now coming into Oldenstadt. The soldiers were all black, not a single white driver among them. I later found out that in those days they did not integrate the Army. Well, these Negro soldiers were a happier bunch than the British. I could see why England was bombed by the Germans and America was not.

We chased these soldiers yelling "Eh, GI, got some chewing gum?" They would grin at us and sometimes throw us gum. I had never tasted gum before but when I did get some, it sure tasted fine.

By now I had made more friends. There was Friedel Ochwat who was Al's age and another big guy with a very gentle manner whose nickname was Menne. He was my age but bigger. There were now five of us: Al, Friedel, Menne, Willie, and myself. Friedel's dad had been on guard duty on a balcony a month ago when he was killed by a sniper. By trade he had been a musician, but the Army had trained him as a munitions expert. Menne's dad was back from a work detail in Belgium, building fortifications along some shores, but was needed here in Uelzen to keep the trains running. Trains were always a priority target, so there was plenty of work for him and his crew.

The five of us would take walks through the town and woods and we came across a variety of munitions that the German Army left behind. We found all kinds of uses for these; in fact it became our daily routine, seeing what we could find and set off. These were our only toys. There was not a single soccer ball in town; none had been made in the last few years because that did not help the war effort.

We got word that there was a cold-storage fruit warehouse selling off fruits and vegetables. Terrific! We got the big hauling bags that mom had made for us, and ran off to the store in Uelzen. Sure enough, they were emptying the warehouse and there were hundreds of people in line already. So we also fell in line in hopes of getting some fruit. But, what's this? The war was not yet (officially) over and here came a German fighter plane swooping down on us. He must have found some gasoline and ammo somewhere, and now that the Allies had occupied Uelzen, the Germans had to shoot at us! We hit the walls, nooks, and crannies; even a high curb was good enough. That guy really raked the town, but during the chaos we gained a better position relative to the door because some people had fled. So, at the store, Al and I actually received some fruit and even some frozen strawberries.

Being shot at by a German plane, however, was double maddening. I felt like a dog that was ready to fight. Just like a dog, the hair on my neck rose every time I heard those bullets hit the pavement.

Chapter 14

One sunny day in April of 1945, several of us boys were strolling through some tall pine woods along Highway 191, when Friedel spotted a large beige tank mine. We all stared at it and then he shocked us by jumping on it. We thought we would all be blown up, but he explained that this mine would need tons of weight or an electric fuse cap to set it off. It would be too expensive to produce it to kill just one trooper. We hid that mine until we could decide what to do with it.

The next day Friedel came to me and said, "Fine" (pronounced pheenay, derived from Josephine) "take that big canvas bag with the mine and Willie's bike to the bridge in the woods." The bridge was old and made of wood. He thought it had served its purpose long enough. And besides, we would have the time of our lives seeing it blow sky high. It was only a foot bridge, so it was no big deal. I was not to tell Al or Willie. Al might not go for it and Willie might tell on us. Friedel had it all figured out.

Well, we went down to the bridge the next morning to set it off. Friedel brought along a German tank bazooka, also beige, with a long shaft full of black powder and solid rocket powder. He cut open its big head with sharp blacksmith cutter-pliers. The front of the head was hollow and the back of that bazooka head had wax-like dynamite in it. That was to heat the tank mine. It had the smell of death and destruction.

He placed the mine on the ground underneath one end of the bridge and put the bazooka in front of it. Then he trailed a long line of gun powder toward a three-foot-thick oak tree. We were getting excited now! Friedel lit the powder. Behind the thick oak tree, Menne, Friedel, and I were flat on our bellies, hands over our ears but peeking out. There was no one around for a half mile that we could see.

Well, the minute the fire reached that pile of powder in the bazooka, the bazooka went off and so did the 40 lb. tank mine. It lifted us off the ground, the grass and small trees went flying past us and pieces of bridge rained down out of the sky. All three of us were totally deaf and by now wondering why we had done it. It was a much bigger blast than we had expected. We took off running through the woods and returned to the village from the other side.

In the afternoon some boys came upon parts of the bridge floating down the river and used these as rafts. The newly-appointed policeman picked them up for questioning, but then released them when he discovered they were not the bad boys. Besides, it could have been some partisans. Nobody knew anything. I told Friedel that I was finished with big explosions. I couldn't say that it was fun. It was actually brutal, more like crossing the Oder River and being bombed.

By the end of April 1945, the Allies were crossing the Elbe mostly unchallenged since German soldiers were quickly changing into civilian clothing and hiding in the woods or running home by the thousands. Most were caught and collected, and then held in fenced-off meadows used as prisoner-of-war camps. On the 5th of May we were told that the war was over.

The Allied forces divided Germany into four zones and our town ended up in the British zone. Our location was about thirty miles or so from the Russian zone to our east. The French zone was in the west of Germany and the U.S. zone was in mid and southern Germany—the Russians got the entire eastern portion.

The U.S. troops moved out of the areas they had occupied and captured because Stalin wanted that region and got it, including the provinces around Berlin. But the city of Berlin stayed occupied by all four forces. "Good old Joe Stalin" as Roosevelt called him, did not remain good old Joe for long. He quickly became very unruly and uncooperative with the other forces. Communist rule was the order in East Germany with no other choice. You either towed the line or went to jail.

It was very much like the one-party system Hitler had in his regime. His party was the NSDAP-the National Socialist German Labor Party, and only the big-shots belonged to it. The regular working stiffs were sent all over the world to fight and die, while the big-party dogs stayed in the homeland to get fat and rule. All teachers had to belong to the "Partei" (party) and carry the big round swastika medallion on their civilian suits. We, as young boys, had to salute everyone that we met who wore that emblem.

One evening, just as it was getting dark in the village, Heinz, the bricklayer's son, was strolling down the street. He knew that the teacher was approaching him, but did not think to salute him. He was still tired from putting out fires after a bombing and besides, he expected the Allies would be here soon, so why should he salute this Partei big-shot? That did not go over well.

The teacher grabbed Heinz by the shirt, pulled him close to his face, and yelled, "Kennst du mich?" (Do you know me?) Heinz quickly saluted but later told me, "Wait till the Allies get here!"

Now that the war was over, we strolled past the school house where the big-shot lived and there went Heinz. He nearly broke the living room window as he pounded it.

Then he hollered, "Kennst du mich?" You could hear it half way across the village, but the teacher never came out. Heinz promised us that if the teacher did come out, he would give him "such a licking."

As it happened, an Army truck came by one day and picked the teacher up with some other party members to de-Nazify them. We had not heard the word before. There were many jokes made using that word, "Entnazifizieren." The allies took them to a type of school where they were fed well and taught about democracy. I thought these guys really got away with their bad deeds! They had taken away our books, our vote, our freedom, and they even sent folks to concentration camps! Just for not conforming. Hitler could not have gotten as far as he did without their help!

The teacher returned after about six to eight months and was reinstated and was even a good choir director. After the war he had both a male and mixed choir, and was again looked up to. But not by me or by Mrs. Schulz, who had lost her husband in Russia. I was just the new riff-raff who was not good enough to be talked to.

Now that the war was over, mom, Al, and I were wondering and worrying about dad and Johann. We made it to the west, but where were they? Were they still alive? Mom became sick and delirious and would talk in her fevered state, but we could not understand her rambling. When she improved, Al and I promised we would scour western Germany for them.

The three of us made our first trip to Hannover on borrowed bikes. The German Red Cross had books with thousands of names and pictures of displaced people. They added our names, but we did not find dad or Johann recorded. We continued from town to town every two weeks and lived on the street by spending the night in a bombed-out building or a railroad station.

Mom still worked at Meyer's greenhouses, but one day remembered Lebenstedt-Salzgitter, a town built in the 1930s, that was close to a giant foundry. The workers at that foundry were mostly of German ancestry who had lived in the occupied countries. My dad's younger brother was placed there to work, and Lebenstedt had been built for the newcomers because they were needed to work in these steel plants. The town had about 50,000 occupants.

So in late summer, Mom and I straddled the bikes and headed for Lebenstedt. It was about 80 km from Uelzen to Braunschweig and then another 25 km to Lebenstedt. We left about 5 a.m. at daybreak. Northern Germany is on the same parallel as James Bay, south of Hudson Bay in Canada, but it does not get as cold there because of the Gulfstream.

Our first rest stop was in Gifhorn, some 40 or 50 km south. Mom was 35 years old and still quite sporty, keeping up with me all the way. The O.D. green allied Army trucks whizzed by us; barely missing us by inches. The soldiers in the trucks were winking and grinning back at us.

Later in the afternoon, on the northwest side of Braunschweig, we were halted by the "Mittelland Kanal," a canal that crosses Germany from east to west. We were told by villagers that the bridge was blown out, but that the steel girders were only a few feet below the surface. People did manage to cross on foot. Only 30 feet of the beams were below the surface, the other 200 feet were above the water. I checked it out, turned around, and lifted my bike on my shoulders and carefully inched across. Once on the other side I dropped off that bike and returned for moms. She walked behind me with the bags. There was no one around; it was as quiet as a cemetery. Once across, we put on our shoes and kept going.

By late afternoon we arrived at Stadtweg 50, at Uncle Johann's house. Aunt Vallie, Cousins Irma, Annie, and Josef Klemm were home. Uncle Johann was somewhere in Russia in a prison camp or dead, just like my dad; no one knew anything. Aunt Vallie came from the Polish-speaking region of Lithuania and by now had become almost totally deaf, so she had a difficult time in Germany. We spent the next day visiting, resting, and asking around about dad and Johann.

Chapter 15

The following day we used our ration cards at the fish market. As we worked our way through the crowded market, a familiar face walked by us. It was Emma Burstein from Lithuania. She spotted mom, then grabbed and squeezed both of us. She informed us that someone told her that we were dead, that we had died at the Oder River Bridge during the bombing. I grinned, thinking of Al and me making it across.

But the next thing she said made our hearts leap. "Your Johann is here in Lebenstedt and works for a construction firm."

Mom and I ran to the site which she'd described to us, ran up the three bombed out flights of stairs, and there was my now 17-year-old brother facing the wall with a greenish cement mixture. Mom cried out, "Johann!" He dropped the trowel as if a snake had bit him and, in a spin-around jump, stared at us in disbelief. A floodgate of tears opened with all three of us laughing and crying – mostly Johann. He kept hugging and squeezing mom to his chest. By now, the nice blouse mom and donned to go to the market was crushed and torn.

Johann kept saying, "You're alive, you're alive."

With all the commotion we created, half the crew came to witness this happy reunion. The boss looked at us and told Johann, "Go ahead, take off."

One thing always puzzled me. Why did Johann never visit Aunt Vallie Klemm in this town? Did he not know she lived there? Johann had been out of the house most of the time since 1941, attending various schools. I wrote the letters to him as mom dictated them to me, but he did not know where they'd all gone.

At 4:30 a.m., the three of us left Lebenstedt for Oldenstadt to tell and show Al the good news. I sat on the bicycle's handle bar in front of Johann as he peddled and then we would switch. Johann, however, was 17 years old now and much bigger and heavier than I, and seemed almost like a stranger to me. The last time I had seen him was on the train ride to the school in the peninsula in the Baltic Sea called Hela in 1944.

While riding, Johann told me what life had been like for him. One day, during class, a uniformed man came in, held a rousing speech about making good fighters out of them, and before they knew it, the students were being trained to fire heavy rocket bazookas at moving targets.

They placed Johann and his classmates – ages 16 and 17 – along the Oder River on the west bank. The orders were to aim at the Russian speed boats and armadas crossing the river. But, according to Johann, the Russian General Zukov lined up 20,000 artillery pieces and kept them under fire around the clock. By then most of Johann's classmates were dead in their foxholes and he was wounded and bleeding.

An old sergeant on a motorcycle came up to Johann and told him to hop on. The bleeding might be their ticket out if they got caught by the "Feldgendarmarie" (military police). Johann was afraid to leave because the punishment for desertion was to be shot on sight. The old sergeant punched him, told him to get on the bike, and pointed out that everyone around would be dead in the next 24 hours. So they sped away. In Fulda they changed their clothing and split up, with Johann going to Lebenstedt in the west. So, in Johann's military "career" he never got to shoot and he avoided becoming a POW.

Johann was quite cocky and had a way with the girls. He told me all of this while I was sitting on the bike bar for some 85 km (55 mi). As we neared Oldenstadt, we became more excited about surprising Al. As we crossed the little repaired bridge in Oldenstadt, Al spotted us and let out a yell. Johann did not stop peddling. I guess if he had, we would not have been able to walk up the hill, as I was quite sore and Johann was done in too. Besides, if we had stopped, there would have been too many boys around who would have seen us hugging, crying, and laughing. Johann stayed with us about 14 days. He checked out Uelzen and the surrounding areas and then returned to his employer in Lebenstedt to hand in his resignation.

In the meantime, the trains began to run again; a few arrived each day really overloaded. The coaches had standing room only with half the people hanging on to door handles on the outside, standing on the bumpers, and sitting on the roof. From a distance, the trains looked like they were crawling with ants. Johann returned on one of these. He brought along his boss's son who owned an old two-row Hohner button accordion. He'd tried to play it, but it was in a diatonic scale and too difficult for him. To me it was quite intriguing, so he gave it to me.

The only things I had owned up to then were the clothes on my back. Now I had a real button accordion, the type my dad used to play! I started to practice and in a few months' time I was able to play easy-flowing Vienna waltzes. Johann, by this time, had a job at an upholstery shop in Uelzen as an apprentice.

Oldenstadt had a lovely old church built about 600 years ago, and was so solidly built that it would last another 600 years with its three-foot-thick walls. The school was about 100 feet from the church and the area between was our playground. One little guy found a tennis ball in his house and he let us play soccer with it.

As we played, a young, good-looking man stopped to speak to us. We could tell by his bearing that he was a former soldier. He wore nice gray pants and a dark blue sport coat but only had one leg and army-issued crutches. He asked us to help bring the benches into the school, which had been empty for a few weeks. This school had two classrooms which were divided between grades one through four, and five through eight. Once the benches were in, he introduced himself as our new teacher, Herr Niepel.

I could tell by his accent that he was not from these parts but from Lower Silesia. Finally school began and I was in a real German school with a real certified teacher. He was a draftee in the Army, not a politician. In school he was a strict disciplinarian. It was like boot-camp. When he called for an answer we sprang up and shouted it out and if it was wrong we were smacked with his pool stick.

He told us right at the start that it would be hard. We had had no discipline and we knew very little. He told us that when we finished his class we would leave educated, not as scholars, but ready for the world. We would know the basics, which would equip us for a trade or further schooling.

One day after school Mr. Niepel asked to speak to me. He wanted to know where I had learned to read and write. I told him in Lithuania when I was five or six, and after that I had been able to attend a school for a few months in East Prussia. So all the schooling I had was a few months in Lithuania and the same in Poland. He was very understanding, and to my surprise, even appeared human, speaking to me in a friendly manner. From then on, I liked him too.

He insisted we work hard to pass two grades in one year. I did, and also read day and night from a very large book – about 1,100 pages – about Daniel Boone on his trail through Kentucky and Tennessee. I was fascinated reading about the Wild West. I would sit in that little lean-to room, under a 30-watt bulb over my bed, read until well after midnight, and dream about the Blue Ridge Mountains and the Ohio and Tennessee Rivers. In this book, I also learned about the fierce Cherokee Indians, the warrior Sioux in the Black Hills, and the prairies teeming with roaming buffalo.

There were also grown-up books by Alexander Dumas about Granada, Spain. I could borrow these books in town. Ernest Hemingway's "Wehm die Stunde Schlägt" ("For Whom the Bell Tolls") was a treasure. But there was not a single book in our two-room schoolhouse.

The people in Oldenstadt did not lose much in the war. The canons made a few holes in the roofs and blew up a few apartments, but not a single house was leveled. The bombs flattened mainly the cities. Winter came and with it a Christmas without presents or a tree in our attic room. But what we missed most during this time was dad. The times were bleak.

In the spring of 1946, Al finished grade school, also with Herr Niepel. Al found an apprentice job as a house painter in Uelzen, and on the weekends he would line up some painting jobs for food. We had plenty of money, which couldn't buy anything, and things were becoming worse by the month. We had ration cards but were told that things were not available, so we went hungry.

The village pond was full of geese and ducks, but you could never buy any at the store. The farmers would not sell us any. They preferred to barter because everyone knew this money would be worthless soon. So when I got real hungry, I went hunting, not stealing.

I'd call Menne, my friend, who also had a nice sling shot and was as good with it as I. We'd find a stray goose in the little river that was close to the woods, and we'd act as though we were pitching stones into the water, but would actually drive the goose into the woods and bushes so no one would see us.

Then we had to find a way to kill it. If you hit it on the wing or on the side you wouldn't stop it, but a good shot like Menne was a delight to watch. His eyes would blaze with excitement. He would squat down to the level of the goose, which was opposite us in the creek, pull back on the slingshot and aim. When he let loose you could hear the pitch as it hit the goose's head. It would tip over.

I would quickly swim across, naked of course, to cut off its head and hide it till nightfall when I could pick it up. Mom never wanted to know where or how I got it and also never asked me to get more. She was as hungry as Al and I. Menne did not want anything, he just loved to hunt.

One clear fall day, Menne and I were strolling up the river behind the neighboring village of Woltersburg, which had a water-driven flour mill, "die Woltersburger Mühle." It also had a dam and a pond.

Way beyond the outer bank of the pond we spotted a bunch of geese. The surrounding reeds were ten feet high so we knew we would not be easily detected. Our hearts were pounding and soon we were in a good, close position. We let loose with our slingshots and one goose finally tipped over. I tried walking to get it in the shallow water, but the bottom was mud, so I half swam and half crawled across, grabbed the goose by the neck, and crawled back.

Menne was dressed, so he took his knife from his pocket and slit the goose's throat. We departed as soon as I had my clothes on. We did not have a bag with us so we left the goose in the tall grass thinking that we'd easily find the spot later, around midnight, when everyone in the village was asleep.

We cleaned ourselves up and went back through the woods on a trail leading to our village. At midnight I hopped on Willie's bike and sped to Woltersburg. There was a full moon out on that chilly night. I hid the bike in the woods and walked the last half mile. I easily found the trail through the cattails and tall reeds.

As I came to the tramped-down spot where we hid the goose, it hissed, flapped its wings, and jumped at me. I was spooked! It had come alive again! In a split second I recovered my wits. I was really shaking now. I grabbed the goose, head first, and stuffed it in my bag. Apparently the bleeding had stopped and the goose breathed through its slit throat. Boy, what a shock this was!

I took off running across the meadow. I could not bring myself to walk slowly and cautiously along the bushes. I ran along a bunch of fenced Holstein heifers and as I ran they fell in with me. It seemed as if they were having fun keeping pace with me.

When I crossed the meadow I threw the bag across the fence, scrambled over it, and walked to the hidden bike, panting all the while. I then made up my mind that I would rather go hungry, because this sort of hunting was really scary.

Joe Klemm

Circa 1938 – Johann, Al and Joe with parents.
Photo taken for the German authorities while under
Russian occupation

1946/47 – after reuniting with Johann. Joe, Johann and Al

The family photo for the American Consulate 1948

U.S.N.S. GENERAL ALEXANDER M. PATCH (T-AP122)

Transport back to Germany 1953

Joe on guard at the Czech/German border 1954. Sleep easy.

Tank driver Joe with friends Mud Sweat and Smiles

Joe happy with his 50-ton Sherman camping
for 6 weeks on the Czech border

Near Gunzenhausen, befriending a boy on his way to school

Smoke break, driving across Germany 1954

CHAPTER 16

Mom came home from work slightly excited. She thought she had seen our uncle, Albert Klemm, leaving the county office riding a bike. Mom called out to him but he did not turn and she did not want to call twice. What if she was mistaken?

It was up to me to find out by going to the county building the next day and asking at the employment office if they had a Mr. Klemm on the roster. Sure enough, he resided in Bohndorf, in our county, about 20 miles northeast of us. Next morning, mom and I were on borrowed bikes to Bohndorf.

What a reunion it was! Aunt Wanda, my three cousins—Ruth, Irma, and little Gerhard, already so much grown—were living there along with another cousin, Emil Savin. Emil had studied art in Lithuania. Now he was back from the Russian front lines. He hated the Army and the war. He said he would be the first to leave Germany, and he did leave. Emil married my cousin Irma Klemm, and they left for Sao Paulo, Brazil. His mother, my Aunt Minna, was already there. He was then reunited with all the relatives who left Lithuania in 1926.

We received a few new addresses from Aunt Wanda, for she was the correspondent in the family. No one, however, knew anything about my dad.

I began to like Oldenstadt and most of its inhabitants. It was now 1947 and as the seasons changed, I found the area to be quite pleasant, especially the well-kept forests and highways. Many men had now returned from the eastern frontlines and prison camps of Russia. These guys looked like vagrants and were also in poor physical shape. The country, however, was quickly rebuilt.

I, personally, went through a change. I was no longer the tough guy. In fact, I smiled at everybody. The Lower Saxons in northern Germany were a stern bunch, not used to smiling much, but half the people smiled back. I was my old self again. On Sunday mornings I was a helper in the church I had joined. I would unlock the church, put the song numbers on the board, and if the electricity failed during the service, I would pump the organ manually for my friend who played it. This was the year I would be confirmed.

The government supported the churches in Germany. If you belonged to a church you paid the church tax, which, in turn, paid for the church and pastor. Oldenstadt was a tradesmen's village with hardly anyone attending church except on Christmas, Easter, or Good Friday, when the churches were filled to capacity. On regular Sundays, ten to thirty people would attend.

A regular schedule for a youngster was school for eight years followed by training in a trade or acceptance to a school of higher learning. The training would consist of hands-on work for five days and classroom work on the sixth. Al insisted I continue with my education, especially after the authorities extended our village school to the tenth grade. Mom never talked to me about it that I can remember.

Johann had to attend further schooling since he was the oldest, but his schooling had been interrupted by the war's end. I was the third son so I was the least important one. I tried real hard to be important, though. I stayed in school at Al's insistence and also learned English, which was now offered.

The English teacher was an old miss from East Prussia who would ask me during class, "Josef, you're a Baltic German, why don't you have that accent?" I just grinned at her. If she knew how many times I had changed countries and dialects it would take too long to explain.

I was good in the study of the English language. In fact, I ate some good farm sandwiches from the farm boys because I would do their homework, filling in the English words for the German. Each piece of translation cost them a sandwich.

I could not continue my schooling after Oldenstadt because there was no room in the city schools, even though my grades were high enough thanks to Herr Niepel. As newcomers, we were only considered if there was space available.

So on April 1, 1948, I started as an apprentice in the greenhouses in Uelzen. There were two other young boys who also worked there, and all three of us took care of the greenhouses and the outside plants. We worked 60 hours per week and the owner paid us 5 Marks. We were really free labor and the old man made good use of me since his prices were high and a flowerpot went for 8 to 12 Marks. We also had to come in every third Sunday to water the flowers and air the greenhouses.

I liked horticulture and the trade school where I learned the Latin names for the plants and their pedigree, but I did not like working for practically nothing and having hardly any time off. Apprenticeship at the post office, railroad, or engineering was reserved for the local boys.

CHAPTER 17

In June of 1948, seemingly overnight, Germany changed its money to the "Deutsche Mark," abbreviated DM. Wow, you should have seen the change. Overnight we had food, as much as you wanted. Even bananas! I had never seen them before. You could buy anything you wanted. I could see why the businesses had held back from us; now they could sell things for real money.

Each person received 40DM, no matter how many thousands of old Marks you had. I do not know how much money the businesses were getting. In a few months Al came home with a new bike. He was a diligent worker, painting houses on the weekends for extra money. I helped him a few times. We were very proud of him. But when the new money came into circulation, my boss did not pay me for six weeks. When I gathered enough nerve to ask him why, he told me he had not yet received the new tariffs. The following week he paid me the 5DM for that week but not for the other five.

The whole country took a giant leap forward. My friend Friedel was now attending the conservatory of music in Hamburg. On weekends we would go to his mother's beautiful apartment where his dad's piano sat. Friedel played "La Paloma" for me and explained its story. It deals with a Spanish count who has had to stay in Mexico, and how he misses his love that is back in Spain.

He asks a white dove to send his message of love to her. I was really moved by the story and by the beautiful tango Friedel played. To this day it is my favorite song. Many younger musicians have never heard of it. Elvis recorded it, and it was on the same record as "There's No Tomorrow" ("O Sole Mio").

The dance halls were filled now, and Friedel and I would stand on the outside, in the dark near a window, and listen to the bands. Some were good and others bad. We could not go in since we had no money. Al and Johann, however, were dancing with all the girls in the village.

Chapter 18

When I came home from work one day, mom greeted me with some wonderful news: the German Red Cross had sent us a letter stating that they had located Gustav Klemm in East Germany, near Berlin, in the Russian zone. My heart took a leap – life was great – dad was alive!

It wasn't long before he was back home, sitting in his chair. In those days it was not too difficult to cross over to the west. There were no minefields at all the crossing places yet. It was only later that the Russians and East Germans put up the wall.

Gee, it had only been four years since I last saw dad, but now he looked older and smaller. I could see the tears in his eyes when we embraced. Dad told me how he made it through the war at the Russian front lines. He drove our team of horses to the front lines loaded with bread. Whenever a Russian plane spotted him, it would attack. He always crawled under the wagon. One time the horses took off and the rear wheel rolled over dad's midsection. He got a hernia out of it and cracked a few teeth when he bit down so hard. Dad was not a big man but a tough little farmer from Lithuania. Towards the end of the war, when our horses were killed and the Russian army had captured dad, the Russian commander asked dad if he'd killed any Russians.

Dad replied, "I like working on the farm and playing the gromoshka (button accordion), but shooting people is not for me."

In no time, the Commissar produced an accordion and dad became his personal musician. He went to all the parties that the commandant had, and stuffed a lot of food into his garmoshka box. At night dad would give it to his fellow prisoners.

Christmas arrived and it was the best one ever. Gifts were not important because we were all together again. I thought my heart would burst. I would drag my dad, Johann, and Al to my friends' houses and give them the good news. We managed to get an apartment in the village now and even bought a little radio.

But dad was a farmer and he yearned for our farm, which we would never see again. The Russians were demolishing the farms and buildings and creating large, collective farms all over Lithuania. They would declare that this was the people's property, but in truth, the people became the slaves and the big party boys the masters.

So, one day, dad came to me and said, "Joe, we have to leave Europe and start a new life somewhere else, perhaps the USA or Canada. But first we must find out about America. There you can own property and no one will take it away from you." My dad explained it to me like this: "Europe is like a bunch of little dogs, always fighting one another. Let's go far away and start anew."

Al and I were not much in favor of it. We had made friends here and did not want to start over again. But dad said, "Come on, Joe, let's just test the waters and see if it is possible."

So I went with dad to an American affairs office and we spoke to the representative there. That man was loud and boisterous and remarked, "Don't think it's easy to make a living in America. We work hard there and we have mass production, the likes of which you have not seen here."

Dad answered, "That would be fine, as long as no one takes away your home, your family, and all that goes with it."

The representative looked at us a while and followed with, "Alright, I'll put your names up for immigration. It'll take approximately three to four years if it works." Then he added, "We'll see if we can find some sponsors and jobs for you. We don't want you to be a burden to our taxpayers."

Johann was in favor of going and so was mom. Al and I had the same attitude – we'll see.

CHAPTER 19

In the spring of 1949, Johann finished his apprenticeship. He started work at the most expensive furniture store in Uelzen. In those days, furniture stores made and reupholstered chairs and sofas. Not much quality was produced in factories. Craftsmen in smaller shops made most furniture, suits, and boots to the customers' measurements.

When a young man finished his apprenticeship, he went to other shops in different cities to learn their ways and to broaden his skills. Johann worked at the fancy shop for three months, just long enough to make some money for a new bike and for some clothing. He and a new friend took off across the country.

The term for this itinerant work experience is termed "Wanderschaft" (wandering journeyman) in Europe. One stops at a shop, show his journeyman card to the boss, and ask him if he needs a sofa done right now. If he says yes, you do it. If the job is done properly, he'll pay you so much. Johann must have liked this carefree life. We did not hear from him for a year. We worried about him and wondered where he'd gotten to.

One summer day we received a postcard from him from Lake Constance in southern Germany, stating that he was having a good time. Al had also finished his apprenticeship and was now a certified painter. It did not take long for Al to save up 800DM to buy a lightweight motorcycle with a back seat. We both took rides in it on Sundays. It was a beautiful time.

One nice summer morning we took off at dawn. It was an unforgettable day for me. We wanted to go to the Elbe River, the last big river that we had crossed with the horses during the war. It was a beautiful day and I was proud of Al as we rode along the Elbe shores – on the west side, of course.

By now the Russians and the East Germans had many towers on the east side of the river so they could shoot down anyone attempting to cross to the west bank to freedom. Al and I stood there for a long time looking at the barbed wire fence and the bleak east. We turned to each other grinning – we were in the west where the Biergartens were open, and people laughed sitting under the Cincano (an Italian wine) umbrellas, enjoying their favorite brew.

Now that Al had the motorcycle he gave me his almost-new bike. Boy, was I happy! I had fourteen days vacation coming, it was June and I had my own bike. I couldn't wait any longer. I had to see the Baltic Sea, never having been near salt water. But before I could go, the old man had more work lined up for me. On my first day of vacation, he told me to come in and he would pay me my 5DM for the previous week's work.

"Would you quickly go down to the elevator and pick up 1,500 lbs. of oats for my horse." These were 100 lb. sacks. When I brought the bags to his yard, he said, "Just take them up to the second floor of the side building. We store them there."

Never once in the three years that I worked for that old tightwad did I say no, but I was very unhappy with him. I practically ran up those flights of stairs with the 100 lb. sacks on my back. By the 14th or 15th time up the stairs, my knees were wobbly. I finally finished, got on my bike, and reached Bohndorf, directly north of Uelzen, where I stayed at Aunt Wanda's. That's where I met Willie, my cousin Ruth's boyfriend.

Willie came from Pomerania. He had been drafted into the army when he was nineteen and was wounded in Ukraine. His wounds were treated and he was sent back to the front lines. This happened three times. Willie had bullet holes and shrapnel in both arms and also some shrapnel in his neck that is there to this day. Yet nothing held Willie back. He would dance and sing and was always full of life. In Lüneburg, at the foundry, he earned good money. I liked him.

Since it was a warm summer night, I told everyone that I would be sleeping outside on the pile of straw between the little barn and their small garden. I wanted to leave very early to get to the Baltic Sea that day. I unrolled my mini tent and slept in it. At 3 a.m. I saw daybreak coming in the east, rolled up the tent, stuffed it into the bag behind my seat, and was off before daybreak.

The first town I reached was Lauenburg by the Elbe River. I flew right by it. Then I came to Ratzeburg, and by its lake I bought a dark beer at the "Gasthaus," which complimented the sandwich from home. No cooler was needed; it was hard salami and rye bread that would last three days without spoiling. I spent 85 cents for the beer, which was more than I earned in one day. The beer and sandwich were my lunch and dinner. I had 8DM left along with a bag of oat cereal, which, after milk was added and heated, would sustain me another twelve hours. I ate the cereal later that night. By 2 p.m. my heart began to race as fast as I was peddling. I had traveled just over 100 miles and the Baltic should be coming into view any time now.

Another first for me! I'd made it to the "Timmendorfer Strand," a nice, sandy beach with tents set up between willow bushes. I knew at that moment that I would always live near water. The view was endless and beautiful. One evening, a large brass orchestra played Wagner and Brahms at the pavilion and I was impressed. War was out of my mind—forgotten while standing on the Baltic Sea beach and listening to such beautiful music.

This was living, for even if I was poor, I felt as good as—or better than—any rich man.

Upon my return to Oldenstadt, I joined the eighteen-man church brass orchestra. That surprised my buddies and the girls who knew me as being tough and fast. My inner softer side came to the surface. The church provided the instruments and I received a Flügelhorn, which I played well. Since I had experience with the button accordion, and having already played at weddings and school plays, I can justifiably state that the church band played poorly. Nonetheless, it was still fun to perform at church on Christmas Eve and even more fun to play at a farm for a 50th anniversary celebration or some other party.

When we went caroling, we'd stand in a circle in front of the house and play some nice carols. We would then be invited inside to sit at a table and have something to eat. After a few beers, we would set aside our hymnal note books and play some three-quarter-time waltzes and other smooth music, which was more fun and sounded much better.

Memorial Day in Germany is celebrated in November when it is cold and foggy. We would march to the village memorial site, which listed all the names of the fallen young men, and play appropriate slow tunes like "Ich hat' einen Kamaraden" (I had a comrade). One lyric of that song states: "and when the bullet struck him, he fell in front of me; it felt like it was a part of me." People would come out—mostly widows, parents, and grandparents – and I could see many of them crying. But I was content. My family was intact and life was pretty good now, even if I was poor and we no longer had a farm. All five of us were healthy and alive.

As winter arrived, so did many variety shows at the large hotel in town. My boss would make good money by decorating the hall. We three apprentices would run up the flights of stairs with a 70 lb. laurel tree planted in an oak barrel, and we'd also set up 60 to 80 flowerpots for the stage. By this time I had put in two years at the greenhouse, pushing the wheel barrow, hauling 20 to 30 laurel trees up to the ballroom every Friday, and delivering flower arrangements in a 15-mile radius by bike. I would say that I was quite tough, not an ounce of fat on me at 17 years of age. I had a 30-inch waist, a 43 inch chest and muscles where it counted, but I quit fighting a long time ago and no one picked on me.

I was still working 60 hours per week and didn't even have money to treat a girl to ice cream. So on Saturday evenings or Sunday afternoons, Friedel and I would play our accordions and the girls would stand around us and giggle. Sometimes we would take long bike rides to some other towns or places where other groups of boys and girls had fun.

Al informed me that for the upcoming summer of 1950, he intended to paint houses in the village to make some money and I could borrow his motorcycle. He was not nearly as fond of traveling as I. Boy, I could hardly wait!

At the start of this vacation, however, I was determined I would not work on anything for my boss. We now had a "Handwerkskammer" (worker's council) in Hannover, which checked on workers' conditions and if the bosses were doing their part in training us. So, if the old man had had any last minute jobs lined up for me, I would have spoken up and told him to check with the authorities.

I had my trip planned out and was determined that nothing would stop me. I even became stern and let my old self make an appearance, but this time such show was not necessary. As I rode up to the greenhouses in my cap and goggles on Al's motorcycle, the old man just handed me the 5DM.

I was off to the mountain country, the Hartz. I had never seen mountains before. All the regions along the Baltic Sea and Lithuania were mainly flat. Here I was now, on the same highway that mom, Johann, and I used coming back from Lebenstedt just a few years ago on the borrowed bikes. I was flying on the motorcycle, thanks to Al, toward the Hartz Mountains. After two hours I was past Braunschweig. There the country took on a different look. I could see the mountains in the distance. I really was hooked on traveling by now!

When I returned from my trip I found out that a church in America had found sponsorship for Johann at Wieland's Upholstery in Bay City, Michigan, and for dad and mom at Rodeitcher's Hotel in Freeland, Michigan. Since Al and I were teenagers and not yet adults, we did not need to be personally sponsored.

CHAPTER 20

In 1951 I finished my apprenticeship and was making 91 cents per hour. I quit the old man's greenhouses and began work at a large orchard, trimming fruit trees. I had passed all the tests and was a journeyman in botany. Life was much better.

All five of us had to travel to Hamburg for some preliminary questioning before we could go to America. An American post had been set up and thousands of people were questioned there. It was quite an organization. That's where I first saw a map of Michigan. I liked it right away. Bay City was by the Saginaw River, which was part of the third largest fresh water lake in the world, Lake Huron.

The immigration authorities told us that they would do more background checking and would get back to us in a half-year or so. It was now no longer "we'll see," instead, we were quite sure that we would be leaving. Al had had a steady girlfriend for a year now, and was not much in favor of leaving. But to please my parents and to make some money in the States, he said OK.

It was different with Johann who also had a girlfriend. He said he would not go. His lady was Elizabeth from Heidelberg who was smart and pretty. Johann, to be funny, said that he would send us new socks when we got there. His decision to stay made us sad because the family would be split up again, but even over time we could not change his mind.

During this time I had a few girlfriends but nothing serious. The last one, though, stuck to me. She was an apprentice tailor and was constantly telling me how to dress. She would pick on my suit and tie, telling me they did not match. I also ended up buying a different hat because it did not match my overcoat. This, however, was just puppy love. In reality, I was ready to roll! Off to see the world!

By October, mom, dad, Al, and I were called back to Hamburg. The results of the background checks were in and we underwent more medical tests. Finally, after about eight days, we were called in to see the ambassador's assistant. She was a nice, 50ish black lady, fluent in German.

She gave us the good news saying, "I think you will make fine American citizens. Get your affairs settled and we'll call you for the next available ship, which should be right after New Year's."

What started out as "let's test the waters" now became "that's it, we're going." I was happy and at the same time sad. Here was another time of farewells. My three years of apprenticeship and slaving seemed to have been for nothing. It did make a more serious person of me. But that was my fate!

While in Hamburg, Al and I explored the city. We walked the "Elbetunnel," ran up the church steeple of St. Michael, surveyed the harbor, and slowly said good-bye to Germany—a country where I had learned most of what I knew. I was now 19 years old. I had read a lot of books, learned some things in school, and was taught a great deal by experience. Additionally, I had actually spent the last seven years in the same village!

Christmas came and went; it was bittersweet. In January of 1952 we received the message from Hamburg to report there in the beginning of February for the final time. So we began to sell off our household goods and on the last Saturday in Oldenstadt, we organized a farewell party with our friends and relatives. To my happy surprise, my old orchestra friends came into our yard, set up their music stands in a semi-circle, and played us farewell songs. I went out with a bottle of brandy, serving a shot to each. They brought along my Flügelhorn and I had to play with them for the last time. It felt good to me, but my friends and relatives were teary-eyed. My destiny seemed to be one of always saying good-bye.

So on a cold, foggy February morning we each walked with a suitcase in hand to the railroad station. My brother Johann, and his fiancée, Elsie (Elizabeth) rode on the train with us as far as Lüneburg, where they would visit my Aunt Wanda, Cousin Ruth, and her husband, Willie. When the train began to roll we sat quietly for a while. Then dad started telling Johann about his younger years when he hunted boar in Lithuania. He kept talking loudly and with enthusiasm to keep our minds off the parting with Johann. Once in a while, dad would inconspicuously wipe a tear from his eye. The train stopped in Lüneburg. Johann and Elsie gave us a quick hug and kiss and stepped out and we moved on. We passed on almost all the money we had to Johann because we would make our money in the U.S.

Once in Hamburg, at the gathering place, things went well. We met many people from Lithuania, even my Uncle Becker and his family. He was destined for California. All the people who ran from the Russians and were now living in Germany were called displaced persons, "DPs." We were given English lessons mornings and afternoons, which were easy for me. I enjoyed hearing the language and learning more about life in America.

Weeks passed at the gathering place and we made new friends and acquaintances. Finally, in early March of 1952, we boarded a train bound for Bremerhaven. It was chartered and it hauled 1,600 of us. By afternoon, we spotted our ship. It was a gray troop carrier and looked quite small to me. How would all 1,600 of us fit in it?

The "General Taylor" had unloaded fresh troops from the States, and now we were the working crew bound for the States. Al and I ended up in the mess hall and kitchen. We had a nice, friendly, black kitchen chief who told us what to do and how he wanted it done. Since I was the only one out of the 36-person help staff who spoke English, I became his personal helper and I enjoyed the work. Al was sending the stainless steel dishes – square five-compartment trays – through the push-through dishwasher. On the other end was a man who carried them in a heavy, hot stack to be distributed. The passengers could not go to the mess hall whenever they felt like it. Loudspeakers told them when it was their deck's turn. Everything was done in a military fashion.

I really liked my job. I had to stand by the door and click the counter in my hand as the people entered. The Navy had to log the number of people eating at each meal. I felt like a host and clicked along with a friendly greeting for everyone who entered.

We quickly discovered how so small ship could hold so many. Our quarters were tiny. We were not exactly touching one another like sardines, but it was tight. Our bunks were made of steel and spring wire and were stacked five to six bunks high, starting at the floor and going all the way to the ceiling. Our noses almost touched the canvas above, but we were comfortable, and fresh air was pumped in around the clock. Then we heard the big engines revving up and we were underway. The next morning we were able to go on deck and see the white cliffs of Dover disappearing in the distance. The sailing was very smooth; it was a real pleasure to hear the engines rumble in their low, steady tone.

Things were to change soon, but for now we fell into our routine of work and visiting with friends. Young men with bright faces, curiosity, and anticipation of the U.S. could be found on the top deck of the ship. The women lived on different decks and had a roped-off section of the top deck. There was also a special group from some part of Russia. They looked so sad and had hollow eyes and ashen faces. They all wore the same type of clothing, donated by the U.S., and they never spoke a word. They were fed somewhere else because I never saw them in our mess hall. The word was that the U.S. freed them from a prison in some Communist country.

We were now on the Atlantic in international waters. The speakers were turned on and a Navy guy announced that the canteen was now open. A carton of cigarettes sold for 99 cents. Wow, ½ cent per cigarette! All of us ran to the canteen and each bought a carton. I did not smoke, but for that price I had to start. I got a carton of Phillip Morris, Al a carton of Old Golds. Other guys acted as though they already knew the American brands and asked for the long Pall Malls. A few minutes later we were all on deck, each of us lighting a cigarette. I was coughing but puffing away. I did not know any better.

The first few days of the North Atlantic crossing were a real pleasure. There were porpoises trailing us at times, other times surfing close to the ship in the front wake. Soon gray, dark clouds appeared and the swells grew, slowly lifting and lowering the ship, which made some people seasick. We, Al and I, felt fine, did our jobs in the mess hall, and kept grinning. Charlie, the mess chief, would tell me about his dreams of the Frauleins who worked in the mess hall. Al and I were not looking for girls then. Instead, we wanted to find out more about the U.S.

By now the swells turned into huge waves and the ship heaved up and down like a seesaw. The waves became higher than the ship, but I knew that this vessel had crossed the ocean many times and was built of steel. All the hatches and doors were battened down and locked. No one was allowed on deck, but Al and I could go on deck, or at least peek at it from our mess hall service stairs.

Wow, what a scene! The deck had ropes tied criss-cross all over the top deck. If one were to attempt walking out, one would be swept overboard in a minute. When those huge waves came crashing down onto the front deck, the back of the ship would climb out of the water. The minute the propeller lifted out of the water, we could hear the big diesels speeding up. Then, when the front end rose, the propellers would hit the water at great speed and that would make the ship shudder and shake. This tumult lasted for a day.

Charlie told me that the ship was not equipped with a propeller brake. The storm would continue for another three days, and the engines might have to be turned off to keep them from revving up too high. The mariners ended up doing just that, leaving the ship to bob like a cork and weave from side to side.

As I walked down to the men's room I was shocked. The usually scrubbed and clean-smelling room now looked and smelled like a disaster. The water was ankle-deep, having spilled from the urinals and toilets. As the ship heaved to and fro, so did the contents of the spilled toilets, hitting one wall then the other, splashing everything up to the ceiling. This would then drip on you. Try and sit on a stool!

As I was climbing down the stairs to the mess hall, I met what was, at one time, a pretty young lady. She was now a sick-looking messy girl, holding on to the railing with one hand and the metal step on which she was sitting, with the other. She wore a beautiful brown fur coat on which she had vomited all over.

Al sat at a table in the mess hall. Our grins were not as wide now and we looked a bit strained too. Al had seen mom on the top deck and said that she was still fine, but had had no appetite during the last couple of days. She told him that dad was quite seasick, his bunk being way in the front of the ship. He was living on pills and water.

During this storm, the mess hall still smelled of good food and we kept everything scrubbed and clean. I stood by the door, holding on to the rail with one hand while counting with the clicker in the other. We had the tastiest short pork ribs and sauerkraut. A few people made it to the door, but when they smelled the food they became sick. I would pass out plastic bags to them as they went back up the stairs.

On days like this, we would feed only 300 to 400 people with approximately 1,200 being sick. We then had to dump all those 100-gallon barrels of sauerkraut and ribs into the ocean. I could have cried. But the Navy cooks for everyone and does not keep leftovers. In New York more supplies were waiting for the return trip, and the ship's coolers had better be empty and clean.

Finally, after three days of bobbing up and down and heaving sideways and every which way, it was safe enough to start up the big diesels. Slowly we continued our trip to America.

Chapter 21

As the storm subsided, I could hear the diesels running at full speed. We could walk across the mess hall without holding on to anything, and the food trays were not flying into the walls anymore. We stayed busy cleaning up the ship and ourselves.

Now I pondered, "How did the Pilgrims survive a storm like this in their little wooden ships and how many sank?" Charlie told me that in good weather the crossing took eight to nine days. Well, we were not that lucky. On the day the ropes were removed we could finally get out on deck and enjoy a few glimpses of the sun. It sure was wonderful and did that sunlight ever feel good!

In the early morning of our 13th day at sea, as I stood on deck, the seagulls greeted me. The ship was sailing smoothly and I could actually glimpse land. All excited, I ran downstairs to get Al. He had not finished his job, but I pulled him up on deck telling him we'd take care of the chores later. We had to see this: in the far distance we began to observe what seemed to be New York. Then, to the west of us, rising slowly above the horizon, we saw it. There, in all its glory, was the Statue of Liberty!!!

In all of my life, after many ups and downs and exciting moments, this particular instant is etched in my mind forever. Here are Al and I, standing on a troop carrier, looking wide-eyed, in awe, at the statue, realizing that we made it all the way to the west! We both had lumps in our throats and wondered what the future held for us here, in this big country.

By now, the deck was full of people. To the east of us was the city of New York. There was a four or six lane highway along Manhattan Island with cars bumper to bumper. I had never seen so many cars in my life. There must be a lot of rich people here to own so many cars, I thought! And the cars were of colors other than black and gray. There were some with black bodies and white roofs and vice versa. All the colors you could imagine! Al and I swore to ourselves that we would also have a car, no matter what it would take.

We docked at Pier 73 on Manhattan Island. Everything went quickly and smoothly in a military manner. As we went down the gangway, the longshoremen threw our suitcases on the buses. We were not allowed to touch them yet. We were driven through Manhattan to Central Station. Our necks were already hurting from all the upward straining to see the skyscrapers. Once at the Station, my eyes widened again. I had never seen such a grand building!

Then we came to the volunteer church ladies. Lutherans were told to line up in one place, Catholics in another, and Jews in a third. We received a cup of coffee and a doughnut and they pinned a travel ticket on us, like we were baggage. Our destination was Bay City, Michigan. We were guided onto a nice New York Central train, and before long, we were traveling along the Hudson River.

It was a long trip. My last new shipboard friend got off in Rochester, NY. It seemed that the night would never end, but finally we arrived in Detroit at Union Station. It was morning and here were the ladies again: more doughnuts and coffee. We had not eaten a real meal since the last morning in New York. The ladies ushered us onto a single trolley-like train with a diesel engine.

Now we traveled at a snails pace, going straight north. Some people left the train in Flint and the last group in Saginaw. That left the four of us all alone on this slow-moving wagon. As we left Saginaw, I asked the porter if Bay City was next.

He said, "Yes, and it is also the end of the line."

My heart sank a bit. The countryside that we were now crossing reminded me of the last place in Lithuania: all marshes and muddy fields. We were traveling on the west side of the Saginaw River and the stretch between Saginaw and Bay City is just that—all marshes.

But as we approached Bay City, I became happier. We crossed Salzburg Street, which was blacktopped and dry. Besides, my grandmother was born in Salzburg, Austria, so the name of the street raised my spirits. A few blocks down the tracks we crossed another main street. This one was called Wenona Street, and it had blinking red lights at the railroad crossing. I liked all the trees along the street that overlooked the Saginaw River. Finally we crossed the river and came to a stop on the other side. This was it. This was our destination!

A nice gentleman was waiting for us. He introduced himself as Mr. Matthew Wieland (Matt). He spoke the outdated German of 100 years ago, but we understood him well. Since it was now noon on Sunday, he explained that our pastor, Mr. Herman Zehnder, could not pick us up. He held three Sunday services so Mr. Wieland took his place and drove us to Freeland, to our parents' sponsor, the Rodeitcher Hotel and Chinese Restaurant. Mom was to work in the kitchen and motel, and dad was to take care of the Rodeitcher farm on Garfield Road.

Mr. Wieland asked us if Al and I wanted to work for him at his Upholstery Company in Bay City. Originally, my brother Johann was supposed to have worked there, but since he did not come with us, Mr. Wieland asked us instead. We said yes, and he said he would pick us up at seven in the morning. Then, he left. Mrs. Rodeitcher came to greet us and said she would see us as soon as she was done with the guests in the dining room. So here we sat, on our four suitcases in the reception hall, from noon until three, staring at the walls.

The doughnuts from yesterday morning in New York and this morning in Detroit were long digested and we were hungry. We waited, not knowing what else to do. At three she came and asked us if we wanted some hamburgers. Definitely! So that's how our first two days in America went.

Mr. Wieland picked us up early the next morning, stopping at White's Drive-In on Euclid Ave. for, guess what, coffee and doughnuts! His upholstery shop was big and modern, and was next to a new furniture store that had a big carpet selection upstairs. We were paid 75 cents per hour, which was good at that time; besides, we were only just learning about upholstering. I liked it better than the greenhouse business, with the long hours six days per week, and even Sundays when the flowers needed care. At the Do-All Upholstery we took off on Friday afternoon and did not return until Monday morning.

Gasoline was selling for 24 cents a gallon for regular—much cheaper than it had been in Germany. Mr. Wieland picked us up every morning Monday through Friday for three weeks. He surely was a nice man and went out of his way for Al and myself.

One day he said, "Boys, let's go to the Sheriff's Office on Center Avenue. You have to get your own driver's licenses."

We each had a German Class 4 driver's license good for motorcycles and slow-moving tractors. Mr. Wieland told the lady at the Sheriff's Office that our English was not that good. Could he ask us the questions in German since we already knew the traffic signs? She replied that was a bit unusual but to go ahead.

We walked out of there with our licenses and that same day, at quitting time, Mr. Wieland said, "Take my station wagon to Freeland. See you tomorrow."

Wow! Here we were, just three weeks in the U.S.A. and were driving ourselves down Salzburg Road, the one we crossed by train coming into Bay City.

On one beautiful Saturday morning in April 1952, mom's first weekend off from the kitchen, we all got into Mr. Wieland's station wagon. We rolled slowly along the Tittabawassee River to Saginaw, parked the car on Genessee St., and strolled along, window-shopping in the beautiful downtown district. Dad and mom looked for an American suit for dad, while Al and I went into Kresge's for ice cream. The sundaes were rich and creamy with real strawberries and only cost pennies.

The beautiful girl with long blond hair and blue eyes behind the counter wanted to know where we came from. She told us she was from Berlin and had a brother named Achim. Achim had two friends, one from Austria, Martin, and the other, Adam, from Hungary. We gave her our address in Freeland and that same night the three guys came over to visit us. We became friends right away. These three had come to the States in 1951; they had cars and jobs. All were of German descent so we listened to many of their German records and stuck together from then on. It was surely nice to have friends because for the first six weeks we were lonesome and lost. They were all 20 years old, the same as Al.

Going to church every Sunday morning was a must for us because that's where we met many other immigrants from the eastern European countries. They all had ancestors dating back to the days of Catherine the Great, who had brought Germans into Russia and other eastern countries, to teach the natives skills that were sorely needed to modernize their infrastructure. These Germans were transplanted into the regions from Estonia in the north to Romania and the Black Sea in the south. After the Communists took over in 1939 and again in 1944 and 1945, these people were chased all over Western Europe and finally made a new start here in America, thanks to the open-door policy of the U.S.

We were all eager to work and succeed and not be dependent on the government. And succeed we did. Pastor Hermann Zehnder at Zion Lutheran Church in Bay City was my pastor and friend. He was about 16 years older than I, but we understood one another well. He talked and joked with me and I liked his sermons. He never pretended to be holier than anyone else. He had two brothers in Frankenmuth, Michigan. One ran the

Zehnder's Inn and "Tiny" Zehnder with his wife, Dorothy, had the Bavarian Inn. Through the years I became friends with Tiny's family also.

At the end of April, Mr. Wieland took Al and myself to Mr. Labadie's used car lot on Lafayette Street. He told us that Mr. Labadie was an honest man and selling used cars was all he knew. Al and I did not think that we were financially able to buy a car, but Mr. Wieland said, "Let's go and see." Mr. Labadie showed us all kinds of ten-year-old cars. Al and I stopped at a 1941 dark blue Buick. It had a straight eight-cylinder engine, the size of a ship's engine, and a short muffler with a good, low sound that turned us on. Mr. Wieland doled out $300, a loan, and we drove it off the lot. As we got back to the shop, Cliff Wieland, the youngest Wieland boy, asked me, "What did you get?"

I said, "A 1941 Buick eight-cylinder."

He grinned and said, "All Buicks are eight cylinder; just say, a Buick." Well, I pointed at the hood where it said "Buick Eight," and Cliff said that was for people who didn't know. I learned a lot from Cliff. He was a nice, intelligent, young man. He designed the new styles of sofas and chairs, and Mr. Wieland was planning to produce them en masse.

So, on this evening, Al and I drove to Freeland with our own Buick. You should have seen our parents' proud looks. Now we were independent.

On Easter morning, mom's day off, we all put on our new suits and drove to church in Bay City for the Easter Service. It was sunny, bright, and warm. The church was decked out with fragrant hyacinths and beautiful Easter lilies. After church, we took our parents for a ride along Saginaw Bay to Bay City State Park. We all felt so close and happy; no one said a word as we just listened to the motor purr along Lake Huron's Saginaw Bay.

The Monday after Easter, Al and I found a nice apartment with two bedrooms in Bay City. Living at our motel was expensive and my parents just broke even. So we packed our four suitcases, put them in the Buick, and moved. Dad got a job at the Nichols and Foss meat packing plant, and mom did housework for the well-to-do store owners where she was paid $1.00 an hour. Dad was making $1.25 and we really started to save money now. At Wieland's, Al was getting good at making sofa and chair frames. Myself, I liked to be outside. I helped Mr. Wieland build a house for his son, Jim, on Wilder Road. Every morning, before we left for the building site, Mr. Wieland and I would sit ourselves down at the sewing machines and really cut loose sewing a bunch of cushions for the chairs and sofas. I followed his directions and he always pointed out to me how slow the women were who sewed there. Al later told me that when Mr. Wieland and I left for the building site, the women would undo our sewing jobs and resew them the proper way, but no one would tell Mr. Wieland he was a lousy seamstress.

I loved building, mixing mud, nailing 2x4s, and painting.

On one beautiful, sunny Sunday morning as I was sitting in church, I spotted a couple of little girls with typical German pigtails. At their side sat an older girl, about 17, with a modern hairdo. Typically, after the service, all the immigrants would gather outside and exchange the news of the week. I stepped away from the crowd and waited for the girl with the modern haircut to walk by.

As she approached, I greeted her and asked, "Have you been here long?"

"No," she said, "just a few weeks. I sew all week in the knitting mill and hang around on weekends like a zombie, not knowing any English. I don't know anyone here and wish I were back in my village in Germany."

"Well," I said, "I have a brother and parents here, friends, and a big Buick and we get together, listening to the latest records. On weekends we head for the woods with our cars, up north to the Rifle River. There are over 10,000 lakes in this state and much to explore. Just stick with us for a while. By the way, my name is Josef Klemm, what's yours?"

"Irma Wiederrich."

"Glad to meet you, Irma. Here is my address, we'll get together soon."

Back home around noontime, as mother was frying chicken and while we ate, I told everyone at the table that I had met this girl from Germany and that she was interested in meeting us. Just then (only two hours after church) Irma came by with another girl, this one from Berlin.

She must have been lonely. A girl in Germany would not have walked to a boy's house. Al and I took the two girls for a ride along Lake Huron and a friendship began. Most Saturday nights, we took them to the Starlite Drive-In Movie Theater. John Wayne, then, was at his best. I did not do badly either, I got to smooch a little. Irma had to be home by 10 p.m. because Mr. Wiederrich was very strict.

Al and I had no intention of getting another car, so if the girls wanted to see one of us they got us both. Irma always hung with me. Al would have a new date every four weeks. Eventually, he introduced us to a Diata Neumann who was blond, blue-eyed, tall, and slim. She wore high-heeled, red shoes and stuck with Al. Irma was born in Romania, close to the Black Sea. Diata came from White Russia, also of German descent. We all spoke German since our English was not too hot and the girls did not want to sound stupid. I did not care. I had a couple years of English at school in Oldenstadt, and I did the talking while buying or negotiating anything for the family, or while gassing up.

One day our barber wanted to know if we would paint his house. Sure, was the answer, how much would he pay? He said he'd give us $100 and supply the paint. No problem. Half of the houses in Bay City needed painting. We decided to paint after our regular hours at Wieland, but we first had to scrape and clean the old wood siding. To the first coat we added a lot of linseed oil and turpentine so that it would soak deeply into the boards. The second coat came directly out of the can. That house looked great when we finished after two weeks of evening work and two weekends. Immediately, the barber's neighbor asked to have his house painted, and we had our second job. The $300 we earned we gave to Mr. Wieland in repayment for the car. He was pleasantly surprised to get it back so quickly.

We had our social security cards and our green cards. Now Al and I went to the draft board at the county building. An elderly (to us) lady of about 40 explained that in the Truman administration foreigners would not be drafted but that we could volunteer for the draft. That would please Uncle Sam, especially since we were at war in Korea against the Communists. That's all she had to say to us, "Communists," and we volunteered on the spot.

The lady smiled and said, "You'll do fine in the U.S., you have the right spirit." We told our friends about joining, so George Krohn and Eddy Prichkaitis then also signed up. Adam and Martin had volunteered earlier and were already on active duty. They had come to the States one year before, so they were a little ahead of us.

As the weeks went by we kept painting houses on the side. The house Mr. Wieland and I were building was roughed in by now. One day, as I was working with the skill saw, I had to cut along the wall and held the blade guard with my left hand. As I stepped back, my foot caught on something on the floor, I stumbled, came too close to the running blade, and – zip – two of my fingertips flew off.

Dr. Campbell grafted the skin from my arm onto the fingertips. During the two-hour operation, he asked me to sing with him some of the German songs he remembered. Mercy Hospital was run by nuns and the supervising sister stuck her head into the operating room while we were singing "Muss ich den," shook her head saying, "What is this world coming to?" and left slamming the door. That made us grin a bit and he continued with his work.

Before I left with the heavily bandaged arm and hand he told me to stay away from work for four to five weeks and to be careful. I was not happy with myself and told him I would not be so stupid and careless with machinery again. Dr. Campbell was a fine doctor—friendly and very personable.

On a nice, summer Saturday morning, Al and I strolled down Washington Avenue looking at shiny, used cars. That day we were not painting a house since I had to nurse my bandaged left hand. We stopped at Whyte Motor Sales used car lot across from our beautiful City Hall. There we came across a 1948 Dodge with a semi-automatic fluid drive transmission that caught our eye. We test-drove it for a few blocks. It was a quiet, heavy, smooth machine with a plush interior. We had counted our money in the Maxwell House coffee can that morning. We could pay cash for most of it, but would need a $200 loan from the National Bank of Saginaw. We left our Buick behind and drove the shiny machine home. Mom and dad were all smiles when we next drove them through the State Park.

Restlessness attacked me – we had to go someplace and explore. Cousin Ewald Klemm lived in New Jersey, working at Seabrook Farms for the Jolly Green Giant. We had two days, the weekend, to visit him. The U.S. did not yet have an expressway system, but at the Pennsylvania border we encountered the Pennsylvania Turnpike. Once on it, it was like a dream. The mountains and the tunnels were beautiful. The white water streams and the endless woods were breathtaking. Dad loved to stop at the rest areas built by Howard Johnson. Bright-tiled roofs and spotless kitchens were equaled by the fast service and quality food. I appreciated all that too, but was anxious to keep rolling to see as much as possible.

Before the weekend was over we were back in Bay City. We took our Dodge in for minor repairs to Whyte's. While there, we met the owner who also had a Plymouth-DeSoto dealership. The new car showroom was on Washington and the service department was behind it, reaching Saginaw Street—all under one roof.

We had a nice conversation with Mr. Whyte, and after a while he asked, "Which one of you boys would like to work for me?" We told him that we were not mechanics and were employed at Wieland's Do-All Shop. "Well," he said, "You can work the grease rack, change tires, change mufflers and springs, plus help my shop manager, Al Gougeon, tow cars and get parts. There are all kinds of jobs here."

I said, "I'd like that because Mr. Wieland and I are almost done with building the house. It's just waiting for the plasterer."

This meant that I would not return to the upholstery shop, which was a bit too quiet for me anyway. I knew I would like the driving and repairing just fine. Al liked the frame shop at Wieland's. When my fingertips were almost healed, I started the new job. Al Gougeon, my 35-year-old boss, became a real friend. I kept my work area spotlessly clean and when I finished my assigned work, I took the biggest broom and swept the whole shop from Washington to Saginaw Streets. Although there was a janitor to do this, he always said he was too busy.

When Mr. Whyte walked through the shop he grinned at me and asked, "Joe, do you want to see where the horse bit me?" He would point at his shoulder with one hand and, as I looked, he then hit me between my legs with the other. That happened just one time. Then he'd ask me what brand I smoked. It really did not matter; we'd stand and smoke one together. Once in a while, I would bring in one of my fellow immigrants and show them every used car on the lot, and sometimes they would buy. I discovered that I loved to sell, as well as work in the garage.

One day, Frank, an older mechanic, had a nice DeSoto on the jacks. He must have been working on the transmission or one of its two governors. Anyway, Frank slid out from under the car, kicked it, and swore, saying, "God damn, c—." I saw he was upset so I walked over to him and asked, "What part of the transmission is the c—? Come on, I'll help you fix it."

In Germany we never learned vulgar language in our English classes. However, I knew a few bad words like s.o.b. I did not know this new word the mechanic said. Well, when he heard me volunteering to help him fix the c—, he rolled on the floor, called the other mechanics and told them what I said. The guys got a good laugh from that one! I stood there, not too badly embarrassed. Al Gougeon then came to my rescue. He grabbed me by the shoulder and quick-stepped me out of the circle. "Come here, Joe, let me talk to you," and "Back to work, you guys."

These were carefree times for Al and me. We enjoyed traveling and seeing the north of Michigan in the fall where the colors are more vivid than in Europe. Winter came and we had some good parties at our apartment. Irma was still sticking with me, making sure I didn't go out with anyone else. Before we realized it, the first year in America was over.

CHAPTER 22

It was in March of 1953 that a terrible tornado passed through Flint and over sixty people were killed. Tornados were new for us, never having experienced any in Europe. The storms in general seemed stronger here than in Germany.

Once in a while, I would drive along the west side of the Saginaw River, especially down Arbor Street. It was just a gravel street then, but it had attracted me ever since I first saw it coming into Bay City on the train. I liked the location. One day as I was cruising along the street, I saw a "For Sale" sign on the corner of Arbor and Osage. The house looked awful and needed a lot of work, but the frame was fine and it had a basement. Its chief attraction was its location along the river. I brought mom, dad and Al there to check it out and we inquired about the price. The owners wanted over $5,000. We had saved $1,000 so far, so that ended up being our 20% down-payment. We were elated to finally have our own home, something we hadn't experienced since back in 1939 when we had to leave our Lithuanian farm.

Al and I went to work on the house. Whatever mom did not want, we tossed. We lowered the ceilings, painted the whole inside of the house, and changed the light fixtures. Every week, as we were paid, we improved the house. Dad scraped off the old paint on the outside. Al and I already knew what colors would be appropriate for the exterior on this Victorian house with its narrow, high windows and steep, fancy gables. The walls became a smooth yellow and the gables, porch rails, doors, and windows were now white. It was the nicest, cleanest, and neatest house on the block.

Summer came and we spent Sundays on the beach at Bay City State Park. Just about all the newcomers would be there having picnics. This included the Wiederich family and Irma would come to sit with me. Then, one day, as we came home from work, there was a letter for Al and myself from Uncle Sam. We were to leave for Detroit for a physical exam for the Army. We had been expecting it, but it was a surprise anyway.

Korea was still a hot topic, so Al and I expected we would go there. We also anticipated we would pass our physical exams since we'd been examined before arriving in the U.S. So on September 23, 1953 we reported to the County Building on Center Avenue in Bay City. There we encountered a newspaper reporter and a photographer. They took a picture of all the foreigners who volunteered, of George, Eddy, Al, and me. A nice lady from the draft board and I were pictured pouring and handing out—guess what—coffee and doughnuts. I am still proud of that picture in the *Bay City Times*.

As we rolled south on Dixie Highway, I asked the civilian driver where we were heading and he said he could not tell us. We stopped in Dayton, Ohio, at an Air Force base to use their facilities for 15 minutes, and then continued on to Kentucky. By nightfall, we arrived at Fort Knox.

The first three days were fine. We attended classes, heard speeches, and received our uniforms. Life seemed pretty easy. On the fourth day we were assigned to our regular basic training camp: Company B-65 in the 3rd Armored Division.

As our buses pulled up, all hell broke loose. All the cadres were waiting for us. They literally pulled us off the buses. All of them hollered at once and swore worse than any Russian soldier

I had ever heard. They herded us back and forth with our duffel bags in hand.

They sorted us by size. The first platoon had the shortest guys and the fourth the tallest. Al and I were in the first since we were 5' 7" and a bit. Some of the boys from Mexico were barely 5 feet but they looked tough enough to me. Al looked at me, rolled his eyes, and grinned. Wow, this cadre was tough.

One of the cadres saw Al's expression, hollered at him, and said, "Give me ten, right now."

Al had the audacity to ask, "For what?"

"*Fifteen* pushups, goddammit, and count them out loud." When Al had finished ten the cadre said, "I can't hear you, start all over and count like you got a pair and I don't mean like a woman." Well, we quit grinning for a time and went along with the charade.

The next day we were up at 5 a.m. for the three S's: s—, shower, and shave. Then it was stand at parade, rest in the chow line, stand at attention, go forward a step at a time till you came to the chin-up bar, do six pull-ups, and run into the mess hall. For each pull-up palms forward you failed to do, you did six push-ups instead. The rest of the group had to wait until you finished before they could go on.

Al and I were used to hard work and standing on ladders. We were running and walking all our lives. So to us this was a nice morning exercise. By 6 a.m. we had our field packs strapped to our backs, the ammo belt with water canteen fitted, and were marching up "Wilson Hill." They would run us up and down a few times to separate the men from the boys, and then march us back to the barracks. Next, we stood in line at attention and repeated the ritual of the chow line; it was the same for all three meals of the day. Even though it was fall, it was still hot in Kentucky and some guys would get shaky from dehydration.

CHAPTER 23

Sergeant Cortez was our platoon leader. He made Al and me squad leaders, which put us in charge of 25 GI's each. Our English was still bad but we were always the first ones up to the top of the hill or to complete the pull-ups. We did not yell because it just did not seem right to us. The guys liked us and we made boot camp somewhat fun.

Almost every week we would get a shot in the arm. One particular day we received two: one in the arm and the other into the chest muscle. Boy did that burn! The shots were in case we were ever sent to the Orient and encountered malaria or yellow fever.

I think Sgt. Cortez must have been bragging about Al and me to Master Sgt. Masterson. He was black and real sharp and could really chew ass! He was a real man, 200 lbs., with fatigues made to measure. After the shots, the arm and chest were really hurting. So for breakfast 1st platoon, 1st squad ran up to the pull-up bar and here stood Master Sergeant Masterson. As squad leader I had to make my six pull-ups first and then stand and count the pull-ups of my squad. When the last one was done, I could finally run to the mess hall, not before.

So, here I was, my chest and arm stiff and sore as hell, and there is the 1st sergeant with a devilish grin on his face, waiting for me to fly up to the bar. My mind was made up—I would do it, pain or not. My 25 guys behind me also had their eyes on me. As I jumped up and grabbed the bar, I felt like I should let go, but he was looking at my face; so I stared straight across and counted loudly and pulled to six. By then I was so happy that I did a flip over the bar, jumped off and yelled "next."

Masterson – I could see he was delighted – said, as he walked off, "I'll get you yet, Klemm."

Since some of my guys were shorter than I, I stood by the pull-up bar and gave them a lift up. If they did not complete the pull-up, I grabbed them by the belt to help them with the push-ups because we had to rush to the mess hall to eat.

October saw rainy, cold days in Kentucky. The reddish clay would stick to our boots and fatigues. Mornings we had to stand in formation at 5:30 a.m., spit and polished for the 1st sergeant's inspection. Then, once again, up Wilson Hill, and crawl through the woods on our bellies. All that the cadre wanted to see was asses and elbows.

After they had us whipped into pretty decent shape, they marched us to the rifle ranges, where the machine guns and grenades were. Sometimes there were physical tests and other times aptitude tests. I was the only one from our company sent for a German-English test. I scored quite high on that one which qualified me as a field interpreter (linguist).

Since I had never attended college, I was not to translate any written materials. Besides, on the test, I missed one word – bigamist. Hell, where I came from, no one married two women. Hitler would have had him shot. And even before Germany, my parents would not use language like that in front of us kids, even if they had heard that word before, which I doubt.

It was now November and the Kentucky mud and clay became colder. Our platoon leader was 2nd Lt. Bailey, a jolly young man. He would run with us and when he yelled "take cover," so would he. He was always with us and we all liked him.

But one day he was gone – probably promoted – so now we had a young Japanese 2nd Lieutenant who's English was much worse than mine. He may have been good in college, but a soldier he was not. If he would have smiled, I'm sure his face would have cracked.

One morning, our company commander was to speak to us. He stood on the steps of the barrack with all four platoons facing him. The lieutenants stood at the head of each of their respective platoons. The commander looked right and left and then said, "Lt. Saparo, bring your platoon up a step so I can see them better." We stood at "parade rest" as usual when being addressed.

So our lieutenant sounds off like a man with a pair of balls, "One step forward, march!" Just then I had to clear my throat with a grunt. My men heard that and no one moved!! I was elated. I could see a gleeful, little smirk on 1st Sergeant Masterson's face. I think he was proud of my squad. My heartbeat quickened and I began to get warm under the collar. The lieutenant was now becoming visibly angry; the whole company was watching us.

He then hollered, "Come on you guys, move." I knew I would floor the first one in my squad who moved the minute we were back in the barracks. They kept their eyes on me and stayed.

Then the company captain spoke up and said, "Lt. Saparo, bring your men to attention." Now the light went on in Saporo's head.

He hollered, "First platoon, attention." We snapped to it as we were trained. "One step forward, march." One, two, here we stood tall. I was so happy with my squad. Then Saparo said, "Parade, rest" and we spread our legs a little and put our hands to our backs. Sgt. Masterson's eyes were on me and I knew he was happy and so was I. Yeah, the feeling was mutual. Surprisingly enough, Saparo did not stay with us long.

Boot camp was coming to an end and Al and I wondered where they would send us. One dark and rainy night we were out in the boondocks on a firing range for some night firing. We put a white string on top of the M-1 rifle sights to hit the silhouette target in the dark. That worked, but not 100%. After Al and my squads were done, we sat in the ditch with the ponchos over our heads and waited a couple hours till the rest of the company was finished.

Al grinned and said, "Does this remind you of the trek from the east and frozen Poland?"

"Yes," I answered, "but only because of the nasty weather. Tonight we'll take a nice, hot shower when we get back and tomorrow we'll get hot coffee and some warm stuff on a shingle or possibly eggs. No one is shooting at us and we have a happy home in Bay City. Besides, in a couple days we'll be done with Kentucky clay." We sat in the ditch and listened to raindrops, smoked, and thought of Bay City, the sunny shores of Lake Huron, and the girls we left at home.

The day finally arrived when we received our traveling and re-assignment orders in a big manila envelope. The minute we read them we were shocked. We always figured that, since we joined the same day and had the same background, we would stay together. That's what the recruiting lady thought too.

Al's orders were to get on a train and report to the Headquarters of the Army Engineers in Ft. Belvoir, Virginia. Mine were to take 18 days of furlough and report back to Ft. Knox two weeks before Christmas. I would then enter the tank training school in Ft. Knox for twelve more weeks before being shipped overseas. Most GIs in those days were sent to Korea, but I was elated to be assigned to the 3rd Armored Tank division. That meant moving the big machines, wow! But we were very unhappy about our split-up. We asked the army chaplain for help. We had never been separated in our 20 years.

He checked the orders and told us that he could intervene if we were twins, but Al was classified as Health B which meant that he would not be shipped overseas. I was a Health A and I could go. I was happy about seeing new horizons and driving tanks was even better. I knew I'd do well. Besides, Korea was now quieting down, being divided at the 38ᵗʰ parallel, and they just took pot-shots at one another.

The next day Al and I said our good byes. It was very short and sad. I think that was the first time we ever shook hands. We held back our tears because there were lots of guys around. I caught a car going to Detroit, and from there Eric, who was from Detroit and also a member of my squad, would take me to Bay City. Boy did that feel good! We left Ft. Knox after dark. Alfonse Mondoux was our driver; he informed us that he was a hot-rod in Detroit. A young sergeant, owner of the car, sat in the back seat and slept because he had to drive back to Ft. Knox where he was stationed. We each paid him $8.00, so he made $40.00 on that run. They paid us $60.00 per month; a bit more for buck sergeants, so $40.00 was probably one-third to one-half of his pay. Gas was still 25 cents per gallon.

Mondoux did not disappoint us, he drove 80 mph most of the way. There were no expressways yet, but instead four lane highways like Telegraph Road from Toledo to Detroit. From there we took Dixie Highway to Bay City. When Eric and I arrived in Bay City, it was sunny with a dusting of snow on the ground. Irma had just returned from shopping with my parents in our smooth Dodge. I stormed into the house and hugged them all, introduced Eric, and talked up a storm. Mom wanted to know why Al wasn't with us. I explained and told her that he would not need to go overseas, but that I definitely would be shipped out. I was happy about that, but I saw that Irma, leaning in the doorway and still wearing her nice overcoat, had a tear forming in her eye. So I turned down my excitement, not wanting to make her sad. It was good to be home.

Dad was working at the meat-packing plant on Salzburg and Morton. He finished work at midnight and then stopped at Fritz & Al's Bar for a short one and a shell. He had made lots of friends there. Dad wanted me to stop there after midnight so he could show me off to his friends. I wore my shiny brass sharpshooter medal, my Class A winter Ike-jacket, and a brown, high beaked

Class A hat that had a shiny American brass eagle on top. Needless to say, the drinks were free.

Wearing a uniform at home during the Korean War and even afterwards was quite honorable. My dad was beaming. It had only been one and a half years ago that we had crossed Salzburg Road as immigrants on the slow train. Now I was home and it still looked good to me, especially Arbor Street by the Saginaw River. That was my peaceful haven.

Furlough was over much too soon and I was back at Ft. Knox at the tank training school. We were called the Buddy-Pack Platoons, a term some general had dreamed up. You got to pick a buddy from your state or from basic training. A platoon sergeant and an officer were assigned and all of you went through the training process together and would be shipped overseas together as a well-functioning unit.

Each GI was trained in all five positions on our new Sherman tank; they were: tank commander, radio operator/loader, gunner, assistant driver/machine gunner, and driver. I ended up as the driver—perfect! It cost about $12,000 per man to train a tank driver.

The entire experience was a lot of fun for me, especially when I lowered myself into the driver's seat of that 50-ton beauty. It was built mostly in Michigan. The 960-hp V-12 was built in Muskegon by Continental, the 23-gal. transmission was built by Buick, the 90-mm cannon by Oldsmobile, and the body by Chrysler. When I sat at the controls, I knew that machine was built for me. I would go through the starting procedure and then take off. No more Wilson Hill on foot! Those 50 tons could climb it and more.

The maintenance was a bit tedious, though. In the infantry we cleaned our rifles and removed the dirt from our boots. Here we had to clean the machine guns, the 90-mm gun, the air filters, and most importantly the tracks, which were packed with red Kentucky clay. If the clay was not removed, it would be frozen in the tracks in the morning and the tank would not move. But all that work was nothing compared to the "high" I had the minute I was moving it out or going across country.

By this time army life was much easier, more like going to school. So, about every 14 days, we would all pitch in for a driver with a fast car and hurry home. We'd be back in time to stand in formation Monday morning at 5:30 a.m. Our weekend passes would only allow us to go within 75 miles of Ft. Knox. Bay City was just a bit over 500 miles. We always took that chance, however.

Over the Christmas holiday we did not get a pass; I don't know the reason. At 10 p.m. Christmas Eve we turned off the lights in our barrack, but someone left the radio on, and it played Christmas carols like "White Christmas" and "I'll be Home for Christmas." We lay in our bunks in silence until finally, Ron Rondeo turned it off. No one complained. I could feel the loneliness in that place, but sleep is a great help and a relief for a tired soldier.

Chapter 24

In February 1954, we had our traveling orders. Boy was I happy! Our platoon of about 30 men was assigned to Germany. The rest of the 1,000 men were sent to Tacoma, Washington, some to Alaska, but most to Korea. I was able to go to Bay City for a few nights where I told my parents and Irma the happy news.

Again I could see Irma getting sad. We sat outside in my car and she wouldn't stop crying. She said she would surely lose me to one or all the German girls. Her tears were genuine. Here she knew relatively few boys, so she really attached herself to me and I did like her a lot. After a long time of this crying, and when I couldn't take anymore, I said, "Why don't we get engaged?" She agreed and that made her very happy. She stopped crying.

The next morning dad and I went to the jeweler's looking for a ring. In this country, the girl gets a diamond, the bigger the better. In Europe, one buys a wedding ring that is worn on the left hand before marriage and then transferred to the right after marriage. We found one that both dad and I liked. It had three little diamonds in the center and one large red ruby on each side. Yes, that looked nice and Irma appreciated it very much. I returned to Ft. Knox engaged. I certainly had not planned that. I guess many GIs do it, however, before they leave the country on a tour.

At Ft. Knox I packed my duffle bag and boarded an old four-engine prop plane named "Tiger Lines" which took us to Newark, NJ, and from there we took buses to Ft. Dix. In a few days there were 1,400 troops assembled. A train then took us to the docks from which I had disembarked about two years previously. The last transport on the dock was the troop carrier "General Patch." It had the same design as the one that had brought us to the states, our "General Taylor." This time the voyage was very smooth and my platoon was not used for any work details. They called us special troops, but in reality we were the same dogfaces as the rest of the men, except that more money was spent on our training.

In my daydreams I saw myself walking up to my brother Johann's apartment in Heidelberg and visiting my old village of Oldenstadt and the many friends with whom I'd shared my teenage years. I might even see my horse, Lulu. I was so excited I could hardly wait!

One foggy, wet morning we arrived in Bremerhaven. As I looked down to the docks, I saw many men come in on their bicycles to unload us. They wore the long black overcoats that now looked so different to me. I had already forgotten that workers arrived on bicycles. Soon we found ourselves on a nice passenger train speeding south.

Several of my buddies asked me, "How big is this town "Nicktracken?"

I said, "I never heard of a town with that name in northern Germany."

Well, at the next railroad station we pulled into they pointed at a sign, "See, we're still in the same town." I looked at the big six-foot sign facing our train that read "Nicht Rauchen."

I laughed and told them that the sign wasn't the town's name, the sign meant "No Smoking" and we all laughed.

By early afternoon we made it into Hanau Fliegerhorst, just south of Frankfurt am Main. To our surprise, they took us right to a little airstrip on a large meadow. News people were there waiting for us; they were on the roof of the terminal with large cameras. We had been up since 4 a.m. in Bremerhafen, cleaned up our bays on the ship, turned in the blankets and sheets, retrieved our equipment, then rode all day by train, and were now a bit groggy. But here we were with six clean Sherman tanks lined up for us.

Our platoon leader, 1st Lt. Harston, had us off the buses and fall in. Then he told us, to our surprise, that we were to demonstrate our skills as the new "Buddy Pack Platoon" for the newsreel cameras. They would show our maneuvers on TV back home. The general who originated the idea wanted to beat his drum by showing us off in this manner. Lt. Harston had confidence in us, having been with us through the twelve weeks of training day in and day out. I was assigned to the No. 2 tank which was the old man's tank. He never rode in No. 1. We lined up in front of the tanks after "ready, mount."

The minute we donned our crash helmets the command was "Comm check." Next "OK, start your engines." As always it was: toggle switch over both banks, with the right hand over a starting pump, foot all the way to the floor, I would then squeeze both starting toggles.

The six tanks were howling now. I was not tired or sleepy, and when the engines shrieked, the turret hydraulics were at unhitch pitch. With the order "Frontal attack formation, execute," we took off at full speed and the guns swung around to the front. Then "Wedge formation." We plowed up that nice meadow by turning to "left flank attack formation." The sod was just flying off our tracks when we made all those turns at full throttle. It sometimes felt that the governor kicked back my gas pedal and I think my leg was shaking a bit. As we flew by the reviewing stand, doing nearly 40 mph with our colossal machines, there were loud echoes and reverberations coming from the hangar building.

This show with the new troops made Lt. Dean, the old company commander, very envious. He was really bucking to be promoted to captain but was not captain material; not smart enough. He would hang around headquarters trying to impress the brass and they were happy when he left. Now, as we got off the tanks, we were ready to board the bus.

Lt. Dean spoke up saying, "My sergeant will march the troops back." As soon as we turned the corner around the hangar, the sergeant made us double time across the whole base, just to show us who was in charge here. I don't mind running, but I knew we were going to have boot camp in this company all over again.

As we came back to the barracks, the sergeant told us where to get our mattresses and bedding.

"By tomorrow morning, we'll have a standby inspection. Have your uniforms in your closets, boots shiny, and footlockers ready, so get to work."

"Hey, boys," said I, "we're in the chicken s— Army, we'll survive just fine."

Pretty soon our Lt. Harston took over our platoon and things went smoothly. That did not last long, however, because his promotion came through and he became a captain. Since the company commander was 1st Lt. Dean, Capt. Harston was transferred to our headquarters. I don't know in what capacity.

One day, orders came through for all of us to assemble at the rifle range and qualify with our 45 caliber pistols. That I really liked. I cleaned my Colt 45, the first pistol I was issued. With it came a bright beige leather holster. As a driver, I wore the holster top left on the chest, almost under my left arm.

For days Lt. Dean would have the whole company stand in front of him and hold the pistols out straight and then back, followed by hanging the ammo belt on the end of the barrel and holding that for a while. Later, for an hour, the water canteen was added. Sure enough, when you removed all these items, the pistol alone became almost weightless. That was all fun for me. Having worked hard since I was ten years old, first with the plow and horses; next with the wheel barrow and heavy trays of flowers in the greenhouses; then in the States, changing mufflers and springs during the day and painting houses evenings and weekends, I was in great shape.

On the firing range we were happy to see our Capt. Harston again. He stopped to talk to me when I finished for the morning and said, "Klemm, at the moment you have the highest score in your company. Keep it up and I'll check up on you tonight."

"Thank you, Sir, I'll try" was my reply.

My buddies next to me jostled me around a bit and said "You lucky s—head."

I had never fired a pistol before, but all you need is a sharp eye, make sure you line up your sights perfectly, and then squeeze the trigger ever so gently with your arm as steady as a rock, and you can't miss the target. When I was shooting, I would never hold my breath. I would fire as I exhaled slowly. That worked fine for me.

When the afternoon was done I had the highest score in the company. The next day only a small group of GIs assembled at the firing range. I guess they wanted to see who was just a lucky shot or had beginner's luck. There was a heavy master sergeant, with arms like a bear and a pretty big beer belly. He was from another company and was the high scorer in the battalion; he could definitely shoot straight. On the third day I finally beat him; I guess he had a few beers the night before and while his arm was steady, his eyes did not function too well.

I then found myself on a Jeep with my AWOL bag packed for a week. They called my status TDY. At that time, with my limited English, I found out that there were GIs on TDY who were good at football, baseball, and other athletics. Once I got with different battalions, I was taken directly to the firing range. This time we were hauled in a big deuce-and-a half-truck with a canvas over the box. I really enjoyed the traveling and shooting. I was the only peon in the group; most of the GIs were sergeants or better. The higher brass did not ride with us on the truck.

Now a big show-down was being held in the Röhn mountain region. That is such a beautiful area. The upper-crust Germans were flying their gliders in that clear, blue sky, only nine years after the war.

We started firing early in the morning and by noon I was seventh in this sizable group. The guys were from all over, mostly from the 7th Army, and a large bunch of sharp-looking, non-coms represented the Big Red 1st Infantry. The mess tent was set up near the firing line. The way we were treated made me feel awfully good. Next to each shooter was a small table behind which sat a non-com, peering through binoculars, and reporting the result of our shooting: whether we hit 12 high, 5 low, or missed the target. The targets were three times further away than at the practice ranges; we were competing at the international firing distance.

As we stood next to these tables, breathing easily and not getting excited, the firing line officer would sound off, "Gentlemen, load your weapon." Wow, I thought to myself, this dog-face peon now belonged to the gentlemen's group.

After we ate I left the mess hall; too much brass in there for me. Lying back in the grassy ditch I watched the silent gliders in the clear, blue sky looking like elegant condors. I was also surprised that none of the brass left the mess hall during the lunch hour. It was so beautiful outside.

I discovered why as soon as we started firing in the afternoon. My eyes were really screwed up. The targets seemed to be moving and I could not align by sights. I really f—d up this time. The first half hour was really bad, but during rapid, sustained firing, I inhaled deeply and fired away, growling like a mad dog. I was still growling when my magazine was empty. Anyone could growl with one deep breath for 30 seconds or longer. I made up some points with that, but lost too many in the beginning. At the end of the day I was 13th of the group. That was the end of my TDY sharp-shooting journey, but Capt. Harston made sure I got a three day pass for being battalion high and 13th in the 7th Army that day. Gosh, life was good. I ran into my room and put on my neat, clean Class A uniform and spit-shined shoes. I grabbed the pass and my AWOL bag and ran out through the gate. There were always three or more taxis standing at the gate.

"Hanau Hauptbahnhof," I directed the driver. He took another look at me when he heard my pronunciation. He asked me if I was German or where I learned it. I spoke with him all the way to Hanau. Of course, my German was better than his. He was a Hessian; I learned my German in the east Hannover province.

I told him, "Eh, it's a long story." His eyes followed me all the way into the station.

After 2 ½ years, I was finally going to see my brother Johann and his wife Elsie again. I arrived in Heidelberg early in the morning, but had to wait so as not to arrive at their house too early. So, I played tourist, had coffee, and slowly walked around the beautiful city. How I enjoyed the peacefulness and being on my own. I always did like traveling and hoped that I would get to do much more of it in my life. I had a warm feeling of anticipation as I walked on Mühltalstrasse in Handschuhheim were Johann lived. The neighbors were surprised to see Johann hugging this young, slender American GI, and I was a surprise to Johann and Elsie as well. Elsie was a good cook and I really enjoyed my stay there. Too soon I was back at the headquarters of the 141st tank battalion in Fliegerhorst.

Approximately once a month we would have an alert. When the siren sounded we had to grab our ready pack, get our personal weapon, and run like hell to the tank park. Needless to say, for me that meant I'd be driving my nice machine. We never knew if this was a real Russian attack or if we were just training to be ready. Anyway, the tanks had to be out of the compound in minutes, and as soon as there were two men on the tank, including myself, I could drive it out.

Sometimes we just drove half a day, but one time we drove and lived in the tanks for six weeks; that is why we had to take our ready packs every time an alert sounded. It sure was fun for me driving through Franconian-Swiss villages in the upper Bavarian region. The best part of all this was that no one was shooting at me.

Back in Fliegerhorst, our Lt. Dean snooped around at headquarters and heard that there were a lot of tanks down because of water in the bottom of the gas tanks. So, one day, my platoon was ordered to move the tanks out to the end of our airstrip. He had us line up in a meadow not far from a ditch. The drivers had to take a wrench, crawl under the tank belly, open the big 1½-inch plug, and drain up to 300 gallons of gas from each tank. The lieutenant did all of this before the orders had come through from headquarters. I hated to crawl under that tank in that soft meadow. We were to rush out from under there the minute the plug was out in order not to be doused with gasoline. But he did not think about the thousands of gallons of gasoline that would wreak havoc on that beautiful meadow. Lt. Dean's brainstorm was the pinnacle of stupidity as far as I was concerned.

When the orders arrived from headquarters that the gasoline was to be pumped out professionally, Lt. Dean thought he was way ahead of the game since his tanks were already drained, refilled, and ready for combat. No wonder they did not promote him. I surely did not have any respect for him.

Once in a while the brass would pick me up with a Jeep for different translating tasks, such as children's adoptions, which to me were the most fun. We would travel to the place of birth, eating in different villages along the way. I always liked the surprised looks on the people's faces when I began to speak; they were curious, pleasant, and very cooperative. Sometimes I went to the German courts in Frankfurt.

A German toll officer arrested a German restaurant owner for having a couple of cartons of American cigarettes that went untaxed. I went with a sergeant from my company and after the proceedings started, I translated the questions for the sergeant into English. The judge then asked me if the sergeant was in my company. After I replied in the affirmative, he told me I could not speak for the sergeant because I could be biased. So in came a nice-looking German woman, whose face never betrayed any emotion, but who did a good job of translating. Now I got to see a professional interpreter at work. Anyway, the sergeant lived upstairs, over that restaurant, and explained that he had forgotten those cartons on the owner's table. As a result, the restaurant owner was freed and we later celebrated with a cool beer.

In late August we had an alert while eating in the mess hall. We left everything on the table and ran to our billets, grabbed our ready packs, and ran to the weapons' room. They slid my Colt 45 at me, across the long table, like a bartender sliding a glass of beer ten feet without spilling it. This turned out to be a long trip; it seemed as if we crossed the whole of southern Germany, sometimes driving 12-14 hours steadily.

I had eight tough infantry guys hanging onto the tank turret rails. Their heavy packs lay on top of the turret. After driving all night, we stopped for gas. I asked the men how they could stand being hit by all of the low apple-tree branches. (On the secondary roads in Germany, fruit trees are planted next to the ditches.) They replied that they enjoyed riding on the tank and that it sure beat walking and carrying their packs and weapons. This was my favorite alert; too bad it had to come to an end.

The area around Ellwangen was really beautiful. We kept a gasoline can filled with water behind the turret, at the head of the motor, to keep it warm. Every morning we would wash up and shave with that water. By the afternoon, however, after tightening the tracks and adding oil, that can of water came in really handy.

One afternoon a young transportation officer picked me up after our maneuvers had been completed. He explained to me that on the following morning we were to load our tanks onto a train that had been specially chartered by headquarters in Frankfurt. We would be timed to see how long it took us to load 25 tanks onto flat cars, cross the cables, and secure them so they would be ready to move out. The transportation officer wanted to oversee the approaches to the loading ramp and also make sure that nothing got in the way. I would interpret the conversations between the transportation officer and the railroad facility staff.

We were next directed to a freight yard office. The man we were to see would be sitting at the front desk. We walked into the office and said hello. There was no reply from the frog face behind the desk, not even an acknowledgement of our presence. The man was bald headed with a large beer belly and reminded me of the Nazi party men from WWII. They had also sat behind desks and had had all the power. They were in the party, while the regular draftees were dying in the bitter cold of Russia.

The young men in that office, and a few women, looked up in surprise at us as if to ask, "How long are you going to stand there?" They quit what they were doing and watched us, while the frog face was busy shuffling papers. After a while he started to look into drawers trying to impress his office staff, demonstrating his power over the two GIs.

This reminded me of a situation where my mother and I had gone into an office to get a Bezugschein (purchasing pass) to buy a pair of shoes. That party man looked just like this frog face, he had just yelled at mother and me saying, "So you came all the way from Lithuania to get new shoes? Get out of here! We barely have enough for our own people."

My young transportation officer was more patient than I. By now I was really boiling. I figured the officer and I had been ignored long enough. So, in three quick steps I was around the cruddy desk and, before I knew it, my right hand was around his neck and boy, was his neck fat! I swung his head forward wanting to flatten his face a little on his desk, but he braced himself with his hands and, unfortunately, I did not get that satisfaction.

I did hold on to his neck, however, as I told him, "This is an American officer; you did not acknowledge his greeting! You have *your orders* from *our* high command; all we want to see is the goddamn loading ramp." Then I added, "When we arrive with the tank column tomorrow we won't stop for one second. We will roll right onto the goddamn train. If you park your bicycle or car in our way we will flatten it or push it aside and it won't look so nice anymore."

My officer interrupted my dressing down of this individual. "Klemm, take it easy," he said. To which I replied, "Well sir, I was just getting his attention."

The officer said, "I think you got that. Let loose of his neck, he is foaming at the mouth."

"Das ist unerhört" (that's unheard of), said frog face.

I said, "LOS!" (get moving) and gave him a little shove. He trotted out of the office and my transportation officer was right behind him. I left last and before I closed the door I looked back at the amazed office personnel and gave them the thumbs up. They grinned and so did I!

The next day we began to move the tanks. Sergeant Bridges was my tank commander. He ran backwards and kept his eyes on my tracks as I drove the tank from one flat car to the other. I kept a close eye on his hand signals, since we had a full load of ammo on the tanks, and the tracks hung over both sides of the flat cars by half a foot. I trusted his hand signals and he trusted me. He was a tank driver in WWII, and to me he was a real soldier. We loaded the tanks in record time and were soon on our way along the Main River, enjoying the beautiful vineyards all the way back to Frankfurt.

Did I have a f—ing good time in the Army or what??

CHAPTER 25

Maybe it was fate. One day I was on a linguist job with a nice officer. He did not say what branch he was working for.

Later I guessed he was with S2 intelligence, because he said, "Klemm, when you speak English, you sound just like the Germans."

I replied, "Well sir, I am a German citizen. I just joined the Army shortly after coming to the States. I wanted to be a Korean veteran but they shipped me back to Germany and my MO is tank driver." He appeared to be in deep thought and that was when fate intervened.

A few days later I received orders to go to Frankfurt am Main to the U.S. Army Northern Headquarters and take two witnesses with me. I chose Master Sergeant Lemon who hailed from Atlanta, Georgia and Staff Sergeant Edwards from Arkansas. These two men were friends with whom I had had good times. We received three day passes to HQ Farben building in Frankfurt. The Sergeants were told to bring me back as a citizen.

Shortly before noon I was called into an office. Seated there was a man whose job was to test me to see if I knew enough about our government to become an American citizen. He asked me a few questions that I had no problems answering.

Then he asked me, "Who makes the laws?"

To which I replied, "Congress does."

But he said, "The president does also." He must have been getting irritated with my cockiness.

Then I replied, "If the House and Senate like it and approve it by majority vote, he gets his law passed."

The man replied, "But the president does make the laws."

"Yes," I said, "because the Houses approved it." All I wanted to say to him was that if the president could make a law by himself, he would be a dictator. I thought that maybe we were going to argue about his veto power, but the officer was not in the mood.

He slammed his hand on his desk and yelled, "Get the hell out of my office."

Outside my two sergeants were asking, "Well how did you do in there?"

"I don't know," I replied.

"What do you mean you don't know?" they asked.

"We were discussing who makes the laws in this country and after I told him he said, 'Get the hell out of my office!'"

They replied, "Klemm, you better not have f—ed up this one, because they told us to bring you back a citizen."

I said, "Let's wait a while. Maybe he wants to test me some more."

A while later, a corporal came out of another office and called, "PFC Klemm, report to the court room at 13:00 hours with your witnesses." We didn't leave the building, just sat and waited. Finally, at 1 p.m. the door opened and the three of us were ushered in.

A nice civilian lady was smiling at me, "These are your witnesses?" she asked.

"Yes ma'am!" I replied, smiling back. I was sworn in and all the cockiness left me. I felt so good but I quickly hid my tears from my two Army buddies.

It was a beautiful day and we took a taxi to Gustl Meyer's Bar, close to the railroad station. I was buying. When the one liter steins were on our table I got up and so did my buddies and we lifted our glass.

I toasted, "To the new Yankee." But both buddies sat down and put their glasses back on the table.

"Is that how you are going to be?" they asked, "A Yankee?"

"I am from Michigan, as far as one can be from the Mason-Dixon Line," I replied. It didn't matter to them, they just sat there. I didn't realize there were still such strong feelings regarding the Civil War, and I was sitting with two Southerners.

So I jumped up with glass in hand and shouted, "To Dixie!!" Yes sir, we hit it off then and stayed until closing time, sometime around five in the morning. To me, these two were fine southern gentlemen. But being in the Army, I thought that they would feel as if they were in one nation under God. But, as I found out, one can love the country, but still bitch if you feel like bitching (just don't do it too often).

Chapter 26

After I returned to headquarters, I was allowed to visit Oldenstadt, the village of my teenage years. My uniform was pressed, my brass was shiny, and my sharp shooter and good conduct medals were on my chest. I also had money in my wallet.

I sat by the window on the train, heading steadily to the north of Germany. This could even have been the same train that brought us to Hamburg, just two and a half years before as we were heading to America. Now I was returning as a grown man and as an American soldier. I was in deep thought looking out the window when I heard two women talking about me.

One said, "I wonder what an American soldier is doing so far up into the British occupation zone?"

"I wonder about that too," said the other.

As we were nearing Luneburg it was time for me to get off the train.

I retrieved my AWOL bag from the rack, smiled at them and said, "This sure was a pleasant and very nice trip through the heather country. You ladies enjoy your day." This of course, I said in German. They sat there, eyes wide open, with hands over their mouths. God, I felt good! I rented a brand new VW convertible with white walls, threw my bags in, and was on my way!

The first visit was to my Aunt Wanda's in Bohndorf (on orders from my mother). They held me and squeezed me and said that I smelled and looked like an American. Of course, they did not have the good Gillette lotion and Dial soap in Germany. I told them that I was an American already. From there I drove to Oldenstadt, to my buddy Willi Schulz's house; he was home at the time and very happy to see me. We strolled through the village, reminiscing about our teenage years. We ran into my former pastor, with whom I shook hands; he however, seemed quite cool.

"Well, Joseph, you came here to show yourself off as an American."

"No," I said, "I came here to see my old friends. You have a nice day, sir." We walked away. While we were at Gastwirt Meyers downing a few beers, a bunch of friends showed up. A lively discussion ensued. They told me that it was much better now to be living in Germany.

Gastwirt Myer broke in, "Look, we have the fastest and best car in the world, Mercedes-Benz, which just beat them all at the Grand Prix. We also have the best soccer team, which just beat all the other teams in the World Cup."

I replied, "Well, I am new to the U.S. but we already have a house along the river and a six-seat passenger car. While around here, people still ride their bicycles. And when I get back, I will get ahead faster than anyone can over here." That was my cue to leave because I didn't come to argue. I had intended to just return and have a happy conversation but that didn't quite happen.

It was different with the women, they enjoyed my company and some let me know that they would like to join me in the States. I would then have to tactfully explain to them that I was already engaged. I think the black convertible and my sharp uniform dazzled them a bit. I was 22 years old now and looked quite different than I did two and a half years previously when I left. I also knew that when I returned to Michigan, I was going to work even harder. I just had to succeed in life.

Back in Hannau, I learned that I had not missed any alerts, which made me happy because that meant that no one had fooled around with my tank. So when the sirens sounded, I was ready and running to the tank park. I yanked off the canvas from the turret, which was in place to keep the range finder lenses clean. Ron Rondeau was right behind me, throwing our ready packs on the turret. I quickly jumped into the driver's seat and in a second my V-12, 900 hp Continental was howling.

I think my heart beat was going about that fast too. I was always excited once the engine was roaring. Ron ran ahead to guide the tank; that was the procedure until we were out of the park. Once we got to the gate, Sergeant Bridges jumped onto the turret. The MPs gave us the direction and full speed signal, and I was "flying" the machine straight south. This alert lasted approximately four weeks and was my most memorable.

After this long distance maneuver, we had to take our tanks in for a quarterly maintenance check-up. We had a large maintenance shop right on base. I was kept busy greasing and fixing my machine, changing filters and tightening my tracks, when Captain Hobbs happened by.

He asked, "Klemm, are you a mechanic?"

To which I replied, "No sir, I just like driving and keeping the machine in shape."

"I see," he said as he left.

By the afternoon, when I had my tank in shape, the captain returned and asked, "Klemm, would you happen to know of a company called Whyte Motor Sales in Bay City, Michigan?" He already knew the answer and knew that I had worked in mechanics. He then added, "I already talked to headquarters, you will report to me on Monday." He wanted me to be on his team, to utilize my maintenance skills as a track mechanic. "You will drive my Jeep or the tank retriever and you will be helpful in pulling tanks from the west side of the Czechoslovakian border."

All I could say was, "Yes sir." That was the end of my tank driving days. The Communists were on one side, and we were on the other side of the Czech border. We could not afford to have any lame tanks around there. It was an interesting job but, unfortunately, not as exciting as my previous one.

On the other hand, I felt like a tourist. The area I worked in—called the Frankische Schweiz (Frankonian-Switzerland)—was just beautiful. I drove in the regions of Weiden Graffenwöhr, Amberg, Wilcek, and Bamberg. In this beautiful area the beer was also excellent.

By now, I was becoming one of the short-timers. We would bleach our fatigues so they looked as if we had been in the Army forever. Captain Hobbs asked me if I would take another three year hitch, he would make sure I got a couple more stripes. I tactfully declined, however, telling him I was going into business with my brother Al (who was stationed in Fort Ord, California at the time). The captain understood and never asked again. Word came down to us that the third armored division of Fort Knox was to replace us. When they unloaded, we would gyro back on the same ships. This way I got to leave a whole month sooner. Wow!

We turned in our weapons, stowed our duffle bags, and jumped on the train to Bremerhaven. This time no one asked me what "Nicht Rauchen" meant. By late afternoon we boarded the ship "General Randall." Since our train was the last one to arrive, all the good jobs on the ship were taken. I was sure I was going to get a crap job like clean up duty. Those jobs were usually the last to fill. I heard the PA system crackling and announcing that two night bakers were needed.

I grabbed my buddy, "Let's go, let's report to the galley sergeant." The sergeant was definitely regular Navy. He greeted us as if we were vagrants.

"I know," he said, "in the Army you guys ate s—t, so whatever you learned there, forget it. I'll show you how to prepare and bake 1,400 cinnamon rolls every second night on this trip."

No problem. We reported to him sometime after midnight and he showed us how the Navy makes cinnamon rolls. There was a large cement mixer made of stainless steel and a list of ingredients you needed to dump into the cement mixer. So many gallons of water mixed with so many gallons of powdered milk added to 90 lbs. of flour. The baking soda and spice were already in the powdered milk. Run the mixer, and then dump the dough into a big canvas basket on wheels. Roll it to a large table, and then roll the dough flat. Dip a 6-inch brush into melted butter, take a one-quart-sized shaker with sugar and cinnamon, sprinkle that over the dough, and then roll it into a long sausage. Divide that roll into one inch slices and lay them sideways; hit them flat with your hand and space them evenly on a large tin and glaze them with melted sugar. Another Navy person was in charge of the oven. I checked them as they came out of the oven, glazed and smelling wonderful. They tasted wonderfully, too. I can't remember if we ever had glazed cinnamon rolls in the Army, at least not right out of the oven and smelling so good.

The galley sergeant turned out to be a pretty good guy. At the end of our shift he would fry us a chicken or duck and then we were off for another 42 hours. The clean-up was done by lowly clean-up guys.

We went to our bunks and hung our large etiquette signs – Do Not Disturb Night Baker Klemm – on the post. Every morning saw an inspection of our sleeping quarters by Navy and Army officers.

I heard a familiar voice saying, "There are two men still in their bunks, are they sick?"

The Navy officer responded, "No, they are night bakers."

"I see." They walked past my bunk.

"Hey, is it Klemm? The only Klemm I know in this Army is my tank driver and the best pistol shot in our division." I looked up and saw Cpt. Harston, who was equally delighted to see me.

"Klemm, you? A baker?'

"Yes, sir, from way back," as I grinned at him.

"Well, keep that pistol arm in shape and good luck."

"Thank you, sir."

Truth is, I have not shot a pistol since and have no use for one. The trip across the Atlantic went smoothly since it was August and, before I knew it, we were approaching New York Harbor. Boy, every GI on board was just as excited as I was.

We had traded in our script money and now had real dollars and real silver quarters in our pockets when the Lady of Liberty welcomed us back. All the freezing and sleeping on wet snow and other hardships were forgotten as we tied up at the pier in Manhattan. There were thousands of tourists and friends waving and cheering at us and we were equally ecstatic, screaming our lungs out. I thought back to the morning we landed in Bremerhaven, Germany in the fog, and also of the dock workers on their bikes and dark overcoats. Now, here we were, in sunshine, with young ladies in light white blouses and pretty skirts waving at us. There was life with Manhattan as the background.

I knew where I belonged and loved to live. While I was whooping and hollering, I wiped some tears from my eyes before my buddies would see them. At such times I forgot about Lithuania and the horses. That almost seemed like another life.

The Army had everything too well organized. In no time, we short-timers were shipped to that beautiful Grand Central Station and by evening we were on our way west, rolling all night. The next morning we were in Chicago and shortly thereafter at Ft. Sheridan, Illinois, at the disembarkation camp. The following day brought the same drill: strip, follow that yellow line, bend forward and spread your cheeks. Blood test, mustering out pay, be careful out there. We were discharged on August 25, 1955.

No one thanked us for the two years we had put in. As for me, I thanked them. Out of the gate we went, no pass needed. A bunch of buddies and I grabbed the first taxi and went to the Midway Airport. O'Hare did not exist yet. I called home after purchasing a ticket from United Airlines. I still wore my Class A uniform with the overseas ribbons on the chest, and never even loosened my tie on the plane. I was very proud of my uniform. The plane touched down at Tri-City Airport and the steps rolled up to the plane. I spotted mom and Irma waiting. I yelled, "Hotdamn!" Everyone looked at me.

"How long were you overseas?" someone asked.

"Nearly two years."

Actually it was just 1½ years, but I was not counting now. The other passengers let me get ahead and I raced down the steps. Irma and mom stood silently and happily as I hugged them; they were not the type to demonstrate emotion in public, still more like Europeans. Nonetheless, we were all happy as Irma drove us home to Bay City. Finally, I was on my beloved Arbor Street and looked at the Saginaw River and its green lagoon.

"Thank you, God, I'm home."

Chapter 27

The three of us sat down at the kitchen table. Mom made some coffee for us and the cake was already cut. A fine tablecloth, fine china, and flowers awaited me. As I sat and drank the coffee, mom and Irma looked at me strangely, as if I had come from another planet. The kitchen looked so much smaller than I remembered, and to them maybe I seemed more grownup or strange.

It was much too quiet for me after all the noise with my buddies. I took a couple sips and told them I needed air. I rushed out of the kitchen and took a slow walk down Arbor Street. The change from the Army's kitchen to mom's kitchen was too sudden for me. There was no other explanation for the odd feeling that had come over me. I had to take deep breaths so I would not throw up or sob. I just didn't know how I felt.

Dad came home from work with a thousand questions. We had a drink and loosened up. The next few weeks were beautiful at home. I bought a 1952 Plymouth, three years old, from Whyte Motor Sales. It was in top shape and had overdrive. Not wanting to borrow money, I paid cash.

Mr. Whyte wanted me back, promising me any job in his dealership, but I was still looking for something different and dad did not want me to take a job for at least one month. We drove all over Michigan.

Al finally returned from Ft. Ord. He got married to Diata Neumann and moved in with Diata, her mother, and an older, single sister. I wished him luck among the three women. He managed and went to work immediately at Wieland's Furniture. They made quality upholstered furniture using mass production. This part of the business was a step up from the regular upholstery shop. Diata worked at Farmer Peet's meat packing plant. They were getting ahead quite well.

I took a job with Dow Chemical in Midland, Michigan. They paid a few cents more per hour than General Motors. I was a citizen now and as the Dow doctor stated, "Mr. Klemm, you are as healthy as a little piglet." This came after a two-day health check-up.

My job was rolling Saran wrap. I wore nice, white overalls and operated a large rewind machine that had five large electric motors. I liked running it at high speed because time passed much faster and my production would be twice the average. The brass upstairs was aware of that, and my union steward wanted to know what my hurry was. I was promoted to quality control, but that would mean sitting for hours and time would pass very slowly. It would still have meant working the swing shift.

My brother Johann and Elsie had two little girls now in Heidelberg, Germany. Karin, the eldest, had beautiful blond hair with blue eyes, while Cornelia was a lovely doll with bright red hair. They decided they wanted to come to America.

I remembered him saying to us as we left Germany, "You go ahead, I'll send you socks." Well, that did not come about. As it happened, Al and I had to send him money to pay off his debts so he would be permitted to leave the country.

Our cousin Ruth, with husband Willie and daughter Christel, also wanted to leave Germany. I found jobs for all of them here, and sponsored them so they would not be a burden to the country.

One nice, spring day in 1956, I was on my way to Detroit's Union Railroad Station to pick all of them up. Everyone would fit in Al's beautiful Buick Super. The train from New York arrived on time, and when it came in, there was a joyful reunion for all of us. We had a pleasant ride home to Bay City where mom had a delicious meal waiting for us. Al, Diata, and Irma joined us. Dad was so happy to see his family united again and to see his little grandchildren. The mood was festive as we toasted with ice-cold cherry brandy. The toast was to a happy, reunited family and a warm welcome to America.

Much success and adventure would follow, but that's another story.

THE END

Did I look like I was suffering?

I am ever grateful for the opportunities this country has afforded me, and never have I failed to appreciate every moment of life. I knew the drive to succeed was always within me and I am proud of all my accomplishments thus far. I live each day working toward the goals I've set for myself.

I've seen so much and had unforgettable experiences while traveling around the world, but my greatest pleasures are sitting in my front yard overlooking the shores of the Saginaw River, or in my boat overlooking a beautiful sunset while fishing the Florida Keys.

Sometimes though, I think of the past, of Europe and my youth. I think about my "Lulu" who never let me down, and all the experiences we went through together. But my greatest love and inspiration came from my brother Al. God rest his soul.